Money and Time~Saving Household HINTS

Volume I of the Best-Selling Household Hints Series

**Over 1,000 great ideas from the readers of
The Leader-Post to use in your home and yard**

Money & Time-Saving Household Hints
by The Leader-Post Carrier Foundation, Inc.

Copyright ©1988, 1992 by
The Leader-Post Carrier Foundation Inc.
c/o The Leader-Post Ltd.

Illustrations by
Yves Noblet
Wendy Anderson

9   8   7   6   5   4   3   2   1
Printed in the United States of America

Published in the U.S.A. by:
Blue Sky Marketing, Inc.
P.O. Box 21583-S
St. Paul, MN 55121
(612) 456-5602
SAN 263-9394

Published in Canada by:
The Leader-Post Carrier Foundation Inc.
Regina, Saskatchewan S4P 3G4.

Publisher's Cataloging in Publication:
(Prepared by Quality Books Inc.)

Money and time-saving household hints / edited by the Leader-Post
  Carrier Foundation Inc.
  p. cm.
  Includes index.
  ISBN 0-911493-15-8

    1. Home economics. I. Leader-Post Carrier Foundation
Incorporated.

TX158.M65 1992   640
                                QBI92-1693
Library of Congress Catalog Card Number: 92-73856

TABLE OF CONTENTS

IMPORTANT NOTICE:

TABLE OF CONTENTS

LeaderPost
Carrier Foundation

The Leader-Post Carrier Foundation Inc. was established by The Leader-Post in tribute of the service provided by past and present carriers of the newspaper. The Leader-Post Carrier Foundation will use their proceeds from this book to provide financial support to educational and humanitarian needs. Recipients do not need to have been carriers.

HINTS

1 Welcome to "Money and Time-Saving Household Hints", this first hint will help you to use this book more effectively.

— Make it accessible! Keep "Household Hints" in the kitchen or on a bookshelf where it is available to every member of the family.

— Use the index! Here is the key to your problem solving. Look under CLEANING for help in cleaning everything from bathrooms to brass to piano keys to silk flowers to wood panelling. There are also specific cleaning hints under BLOOD STAINS and CARPETS and LAUNDRY. The CARPETS entry also gives hints for getting out those dents when you rearrange the furniture.

Grandma can check the index under ARTHRITIS to find a hint to help her write more easily.

Teenagers can look under BLEMISHES, and BREATH to find hints that will help them fade zits and get rid of onion breath when they have a hot date.

Children can check under BANDAGES, PLAYDOUGH and POPCORN to find hints that will ensure painless bandage removal, easy-to-make playdough and fluffier popcorn.

Handymen can look under FURNITURE and GREASE and ENERGY-SAVING to find hints that will help them remove watermarks or burns from furniture, remove grease from concrete, carpets and wallpaper and save on power and fuel bills.

Cooks can check under DUMPLINGS and HONEY and VEGETABLES to find hints that will give lighter dumplings, how to use honey in baking and how to recrisp and store vegetables.

NEWSPAPERS

2 Read the newspaper. You'll always have something interesting to talk about with friends and family.

3 Purchase The Leader-Post everyday. Besides keeping you abreast of what is happening, the coupons in the paper can save you money when shopping.

4 One reader suggests putting coupons from the paper in an envelope and placing it in your purse or car so you always have them handy.

5 When you come upon coupons in The Leader-Post, apply them to the items when those items are on sale for maximum coupon benefits.

6 For a baby gift, circle the baby's birth announcement in the newspaper with a red felt and use that page as gift wrap, making certain the announcement is in a strategic position on the package.

7 Save the colored comics from The Leader-Post Weekender to wrap children's birthday gifts.

8 Color pages in The Leader-Post make ideal gift wrap. For an added touch, make ribbons and bows out of cloth leftover from sewing projects. Use pinking shears and cut strips one to three inches in width for the ribbon and bows.

9 Instead of trudging to the corner store daily for your copy of The Leader-Post, subscribe to it and it will arrive daily. You'll pay less per copy as well.

10 When preparing a cake for baking, spread newspapers on the cupboard. When the cake is mixed and in the pan, remove newspaper and there is no mess to clean up.

11 Crushed newspapers are great for shining windows.

12 To clean glass tables and chrome fixtures, use old newspapers, dampened with water. Glass and chrome will shine and there will be no streaking or lint left behind.

13 When painting around windows, wet newspapers and apply to the glass. Then, paint and splatter as you please.

14 Fill in cracks with newspaper or steel wool before finishing off with plaster.

15 Save your old newspapers for the fireplace. Take several and wrap tightly into a roll, wrap with wire and use to replace commerical fireplace logs or wood.

16 When you change your cat's litter pan, use newspaper for liners. It absorbs the odors and makes the litter last a little longer.

NEWSPAPERS

FOOD

17 Instead of using sugar in your tea, dissove old-fashioned lemon drops or hard mint candy in the brew. They melt quickly and give the tea a clean tangy flavor.

18 The flavor of tea can be enhanced by placing a thoroughly dried orange peel in the tea tin.

19 Leftover apple, orange or lemon rind can be put in your tea. It adds flavor and aroma.

20 The flavor of ground coffee will keep better if you store opened coffee in tightly-covered container in the refrigerator.

21 If you use some form of purified water, coffee will taste better and the life of your coffee maker will be prolonged.

22 Pennies placed under the pot in the drip coffee maker will prevent scum from forming on the coffee and you won't have to throw out any coffee.

23 To add flavor to coffee, add vanilla or almond extract to the water as the coffee brews.

24 Cool leftover coffee immediately, cover with tight lid and refrigerate. It warms up beautifully in the microwave.

25 Freeze leftover coffee in ice-cube trays. The cubes can be used in milk or eggnog. Coffee cubes are also great to place in too-hot coffee.

26 Scum won't form on the top of hot chocolate if you beat the drink until frothy immediately after preparation.

27 Mix a 12-ounce can of frozen orange juice in a three-quart pitcher, add one cup of powdered orange drink mix. Fill the pitcher to the brim with cold water and stir until dissolved. The powder gives the drink sweetness and the frozen juice gives it body.

28 Freeze clusters of grapes to float in punches. They keep the punch cold and add a lovely garnish.

29 When making punch, make ice cubes out of punch, then you can keep the punch cold without diluting it.

30 For cocktails, freeze lemon peel twists in party ice cubes — looks attractive and adds a tangy flavor.

31 When entertaining, serve hot cider and other hot drinks from a slow cooker on a low setting. This way, the liquid will remain warm as long as you wish.

32 Use canning funnels to fill a thermos bottle without spills.

33 To make butter go farther and spread easier, leave butter at room temperature, use electric beater and whip to twice its volume.

34 Soften hard butter for sandwiches by inverting a warmed soup bowl over it.

35 Prevent butter from burning when sautéing by adding a small amount of olive or vegetable oil. Butter alone burns easily, but the combination of the two does not. Vegetables and meats will be golden brown.

36 Blend cottage cheese in a blender until it's smooth, then you can use it in dips, instead of sour cream.

37 Cottage cheese will keep twice as long if you store the carton upside down.

38 If you want to make your own sour cream, add three or four drops of lemon juice to ¾ cup whipping cream and leave it at room temperature for 30 minutes.

FOOD

FOOD

39 Before adding sour cream to a sauce which must boil, stir 1 tsp. of flour into the cream. The sauce can boil and the flour will prevent the sour cream from curdling.

40 When you buy bulk cheese, put it in a Tupperware container with a lid which can be burped. Place a paper towel which has been dampened with vinegar in the container. More vinegar can be added once a week to keep the cheese fresh for a month or longer.

41 Cheese wrapped in a cloth which has been dampened with vinegar will keep fresh and free from mold.

42 Mold on cheese can be prevented by storing the cheese in a covered container with a lump or two of sugar. This also keeps the cheese moist.

43 After you cut a piece of cheese, butter the edge of the remainder which is to be stored. It will be less likely to dry out and lose its consistency.

44 Grate leftover pieces of cheese together. Use for a cheese ball or serve over spaghetti.

45 Instead of throwing moldy cheese away, take a knife or cheese slicer, dip it in vinegar and slice off the mold. Dip the knife in vinegar after each slice made. The vinegar keeps the mold from coming back.

46 When boiling milk, first rinse pan with cold water to avoid boil overs.

47 To prevent milk from burning, sprinkle one tsp. of sugar over milk before heating. Do not stir.

48 Always keep powdered milk handy, in case you run out of fresh milk.

49 Always use skim milk powder in your cooking.

50 Use powdered skim milk in tea and coffee instead of edible oil products.

51 You can make your own sweetened condensed milk and save a small fortune. The following makes 12 oz. and can be used in any recipe calling for this type of milk: Mix in blender for one minute ¼ cup hot water and ¾ cup granulated sugar. While continuing to blend slowly, add 1¼ cup dry skim milk powder. Refrigerate for 24 hours to develop the flavor. Do not store more than one week.

52 Seven drops of lemon juice added to two cups of cream before whipping will cause it to whip up in less than half the normal time.

53 For best results when whipping fresh cream, chill the bowl, beaters and cream before whipping.

54 If cream refuses to whip, add one egg white.

55 Add honey to whipped cream instead of sugar. It adds a sweet flavor and whipped cream stays firm longer.

56 Icing sugar used, instead of granulated sugar, in making whipped cream will prevent separation if the cream has to sit for a while.

57 To stop whipped cream from separating, add ¼ tsp. dissolved, unflavored gelatin for every cup of cream.

58 When whipping cream, to avoid splatters set the bowl in the sink and whip. All the splatters are in the sink and there's no mess to clean.

59 Spoon dabs of leftover whipped cream onto wax paper and place in the freezer. When they're frozen, place in a plastic bag and keep in the freezer to use for dessert toppings. They will thaw in 10-15 minutes.

FOOD

FOOD

60   Whip evaporated milk instead of cream. Place can of evaporated milk in freezer until partially frozen. Pour contents into cold bowl, add one tbsp. lemon juice to ⅔ cup milk and whip.

61   To add fresh fruit flavor to yogurt, buy plain yogurt and mix with any fresh fruit in a blender.

62   To hard cook eggs, place in a pan of cold water to cover. Bring to a boil and remove the pan from the heat. Cover and let stand 20 minutes. Immediately rinse in cold water. The eggs will be tender, the yolk will be an even yellow and there will be no grey ring.

63   Keep yolks centred in eggs by stirring the water while cooking hard-boiled eggs.

64   When boiling eggs, add one tsp. vinegar to water, to prevent cracking.

65   Before boiling a cracked egg, rub moistened salt over the shell. This prevents the white from running out.

66   When eggs crack during boiling, add a little vinegar to the water to help seal the crack.

67   The yolks of eggs, left over when baking requires whites only, can be dropped into a pan of boiling and salted water. When cooked, they are ready to add to a salad.

68 Hard-boiled eggs for use in egg salad are easily mashed with a pastry blender.

69 When slicing hard-cooked eggs, wet the knife before each cut to keep the yolk from crumbling.

70 Bread crumbs added to scrambled eggs will improve the flavor and make them go further.

71 For fluffier omelettes, add a pinch of cornstarch before beating.

72 To ensure a white film over the yolk when frying eggs, add a few drops of water to the pan and cover with a lid.

73 To separate the whites of an egg from the yolk, break the egg into a funnel. The white will slip through, but the yolk will stay in the funnel.

74 If a bit of egg yolk gets into the whites you've just separated, touch the yolk with a damp cloth. It will pick up the yolk quickly and cleanly.

75 Egg whites will whip faster and to greater volume when brought to room temperature before beating.

76 Add one tsp. cold water for each egg white before beating and you will have double the volume.

77 One tsp. vinegar and one tsp. baking soda dissolved together will take the place of one egg when making a cake.

78 If you run one egg short in the middle of a recipe, substitute one tsp. cornstarch and one tsp. vinegar. The liquid in the recipe should then be increased by three or four tbsp. (NOTE: This will only work for one egg, no more.)

79 When cleaning green vegetables, add a handful of salt to the second water. The sand from the vegetables will sink to the bottom of the pan so another rinsing will make vegetables thoroughly clean.

80 A little vinegar added to the water in which you are soaking slightly-wilted vegetables will make them crisp and fresh.

FOOD

FOOD

81 Line bottom of the refrigerator vegetable compartment with paper towels. It absorbs moisture and keeps fruit and vegetables fresh longer.

82 Place a dry sponge in the vegetable compartment of the refrigerator. It will help prevent mildew and food spoilage, as it absorbs excess moisture.

83 To keep a vegetable salad fresh, if it must stand before serving, place an inverted saucer in bottom of bowl before filling with salad.

84 Wash salad vegetables before storing. It saves time and spoilage as they are easier to use when you are preparing a meal and you tend to use them more often.

85 Make your own salad dressings — they are one-third the cost of brand-name dressings.

86 Keep crispness and nutrients in your vegetables by cooking them in a vegetable steamer.

87 To restore fresh flavor to frozen vegetables, pour boiling water over them to rinse away all traces of the frozen water.

88 To store asparagus in the refrigerator, for no more than a day or two, first trim the stem ends slightly and wrap the ends in wet paper towels.

89 Broccoli stalks of varying sizes can be cooked in the same length of time by making an X incision from top to bottom through stems.

90 Place a heel of bread on top of cabbage then cover and cook. There will be no odor.

91 To eliminate cabbage odor from cooking cabbage, drop a whole walnut into the boiling water.

92 When cooking cabbage, add a pinch of soda. It eliminates the odor and also keeps the cabbage green.

93 While cooking vegetables which give off an unpleasant odor, simmer a small pan of vinegar on top of the stove.

94 When making cabbage rolls, instead of steaming cabbage before pulling the leaves apart, place whole head of cabbage in the freezer until frozen solid. Then allow cabbage to thaw and you will find the leaves are easy to pull apart and they are soft and easy to work with.

95 To keep cauliflower white add two to three tbsp. of milk to the cooking water.

96 Before storing in the refrigerator, soak celery in cold water to which lemon juice has been added. It won't turn brown.

97 Make your own celery salt by drying celery leaves thoroughly. Crush them to a powder or rub them through a sieve and mix with salt.

98 For the best tasting corn on the cob, when removing outer leaves save the tender leaves next to the cob. Place these leaves on the bottom of the pot, add cobs, water to cover cobs and one tbsp. salt. Bring to a boil and simmer 20 minutes.

99 Garlic will peel more easily if you put it in hot water for a few minutes to loosen the skin.

100 Store garlic gloves in cooking oil. They will never dry out and the garlic-flavored oil can be used for cooking.

101 To keep garlic longer, put the cloves in the freezer. When ready to use, peel and chop before the cloves thaw.

FOOD

FOOD

102 Lettuce will not go rusty if you remove its core. Bang the lettuce head on the kitchen counter and the core should twist out.

103 Lettuce keeps longer stored in a brown paper bag or on a paper towel in the produce drawer of your refrigerator.

104 Lettuce will not discolor so quickly if you line the bottom of your crisper with paper towels. The paper absorbs the excess moisture, keeping fruits and vegetables fresh for a longer period of time.

105 If lettuce has wilted, take out the core, soak in hot water, then quickly drain and put in plastic bag and refrigerate. After it's cold, you'll have fresh lettuce.

106 Always tear lettuce — cutting causes the edges to turn brown.

107 Cover fresh mushrooms with a dampened paper towel and refrigerate. They will keep fresh for several days.

108 When using mushrooms in any recipe, add a little lemon juice to bring out their flavor.

109 To keep eyes from running when peeling onions, soak the onions in cold water for five to 10 minutes and keep them under the cold water tap while you peel them.

110 Before peeling or slicing onions, place them in the freezer for a while to eliminate watery eyes.

111 To avoid tears and save on facial tissues when peeling, cutting or slicing onions, place a small piece of bread on the tip of the knife blade.

112 When peeling onions, chew gum and there will be no tears.

113 Leftover onion will keep longer when the root end is left intact. Use the top part first.

114 Dry parsley in the microwave and store for future use.

115 Coat peppers with olive oil before stuffing and baking them. They will keep their original color.

116 Trim ⅛-inch slice from both ends of cucumbers before making into pickles. The ends contain enzymes which may cause pickles to soften.

117 Save pickle juice. Slice unwaxed cucumbers into thin strips and refrigerate in the juice for four days. Then they are ready to enjoy.

118 Never throw away pickle juice after using all the pickles in a jar. It's great for adding to devilled eggs, coleslaw and potato salad.

119 A piece of horseradish placed in a jar of pickles will keep the vinegar from losing its strength. The pickles will not become soft or moldy.

120 Put a few apples in with your potatoes. It keeps the potatoes from sprouting.

121 Peeled potatoes will last three or four days in the refrigerator if a few drops of vinegar are added to the water.

122 Boil potatoes with the skins on. Skins will slide off easily when the potatoes are done and you will retain a lot of the natural food value of the potatoes.

123 To improve the flavor of old potatoes, add a little sugar to the water in which they are boiled.

FOOD

FOOD

124 To boil old potatoes, add one tsp. vinegar to the boiling water so that they will not turn dark.

125 If dinner is getting cold, keep potatoes warm by placing the pot in a pan of hot water.

126 For fluffy mashed potatoes, add ½ tsp. baking powder to the potatoes, milk and butter. Let sit a few minutes before serving.

127 To add zip to mashed potatoes, add cooked onion and top with grated cheese or nutmeg.

128 You can cut the baking time of potatoes in half by letting them stand in boiling water for 15 minutes before popping them in the oven.

129 Reheat leftover baked potatoes instead of discarding them. Dip the potatoes in warm water, then bake at 250°F until heated through.

130 Add a few drops of lemon juice to rice when cooking. It makes rice white and keeps the grains whole.

131 About five minutes before rice is cooked, place a small absorbent towel under the pot lid. Continue cooking. The rice will be dry and fluffy.

132 To reheat leftover rice, line a vegetable steamer with a basket-like coffee filter and warm over boiling water. The grains stay in the basket and do not get mushy.

133 Apples stored with green tomatoes will hasten the ripening process.

134 Tomatoes and cucumbers taste best when stored at room temperature.

135 Instead of adding sugar to sweeten homemade tomato sauce, grate a carrot into the sauce. Lower on calories, too.

136 To prepare a quick and delicious sauce for vegetables, simply whisk a few tablespoons of mayonnaise into the cooking liquid from the vegetables and season to taste.

137 Having trouble finding the right spice? Arrange spices in alphabetical order.

138 Put a few grains of rice in the salt shaker to keep moisture from caking the salt.

139 Save foil margarine wrappers to wrap potatoes for baking. They'll be deliciously crunchy.

140 Place unripened fruit in a plastic bag along with ripe fruit. Ripe fruit exudes a natural gas which speeds up ripening of other fruit.

141 To ripen peaches, pears or tomatoes quickly, place in a brown paper bag with a ripe apple. Poke a hole in the bag and put in a cool, dark place. The apple will give off ethylene gas and cause the other fruit to ripen.

142 When cooking apples, a pinch of salt will make them more tender and add flavor.

143 To ripen green bananas, wrap them in a wet towel and place them in a brown paper bag.

144 If you have more bananas than you can eat, peel, mash them with a dash of lemon juice and freeze in airtight containers for up to six months. Use, defrosted, in recipes which call for ripe bananas.

145 If you are storing cantaloupes in the refrigerator, wrap or cover them so that the melon flavor and scent stay inside the fruit and are not transfered to other foods in the refrigerator.

FOOD

FOOD

146 To keep fruit from discoloring, sprinkle with lemon or pine-apple juice.

147 When freezing fresh fruits or berries which don't have to be blanched, place them on a cookie sheet and freeze. When frozen, remove them from the cookie sheet and place in freezer bags or containers and put back in freezer. This prevents the fruits and berries from becoming mushy and you can remove the amount you need, without having to thaw the whole container at once.

148 Lemons will keep in the refrigerator for a month if you put them in a sterilized jar and cover them with cold water. Seal tightly with rubber-ringed lid.

149 A cut lemon may be kept longer by smearing the cut sur-face with the white of an egg.

150 After using a lemon, store the remaining portion in the freezer.

151 If you only use a small piece of lemon or lime at a time, cut them into quarters and freeze them in a plastic freezer bag. They will always be available when you need them.

152 To get just a little juice out of a citrus fruit, puncture one end with a skewer and squeeze out as much as needed. Seal fruit in plastic wrap and refrigerate.

153 To get more juice out of a lemon, heat it in a microwave before squeezing.

154 Lemons and oranges submerged in hot water for 15 minutes, then rolled on a hard surface with your hand before squeezing, will yield almost twice the amount of juice.

155 Soak oranges in boiling water for five minutes before peeling. The peel and all white pulp will come off easily.

156 To almost double the amount of juice you get from oranges, store at room temperature.

157 Vitamin C in orange juice is destroyed by exposure to air. To prevent this, slowly stir water into frozen orange juice and store in covered container.

158 Save tangerine peels and dry by laying peels loosely on a cookie sheet with the insides facing up. When dry, buzz the dried pieces in a blender and use in recipes calling for orange peel.

159 Use a V-shaped juice can opener to remove stems from strawberries.

160 When adding pineapple to gelatin, always use cooked or canned pineapple. Raw pineapple prevents the gelatin from setting.

161 Freeze the juices from canned fruits and save until you have enough to combine with flavored or unflavored gelatin to make a dessert or salad.

162 Rinse your gelatin mold in cold water, then coat with oil before putting salad ingredients into the mold. It will unmold easily.

163 Metal jelly molds chill faster than glass molds.

164 Grease the threads on syrup bottles to keep syrup from running down the bottle.

165 When using honey in a recipe, run hot water over your measuring spoon or measuring cup first. The honey will then slide out easily.

166 If honey has crystallized, place in microwave for 10-60 seconds (depending on amount). It will come out fresh and ready to use.

FOOD

167 When you open a new bottle of ketchup, insert a straw and push to bottom of the bottle. Remove the straw and you will find that the ketchup will flow easily.

168 Save all small bits of jams and jellies in one jar. Melt and use as a basting sauce for ham, chicken or lamb.

169 If you rub the bottom of your preserving kettle with a little oil, your jam will not burn. The oil leaves no taste.

170 If you do any preserving, save all of your empty jars with self-sealing lids. They will seal several times.

171 Add vinegar to hard-water in the water bath at canning time to avoid the hardwater deposit on sealers.

172 When sealing jelly jars with wax, before the wax hardens put a piece of string down in the wax. When removing the wax, just pull the string.

173 If you have a damp storage area, wipe the outsides of your filled canning jars with white vinegar to keep mold away.

174 Use an empty, well-cleaned detergent bottle to store cooking oil. Just squirt the oil into the pan.

175 Add one tbsp. cooking oil to a bottle of cooking wine to prevent it from going sour.

176 Don't throw away leftover wine or wine that has begun to go off. Boil it down by half, bottle and refrigerate, then use for cooking.

177 Buy spaghetti sauce on sale and use as sauce when making pizzas.

178 To prevent any boiling-over mishaps, grease the inside rim of the pot.

179 Add one tsp. of butter or margarine to macaroni, spaghetti, soup etc. to stop from boiling over.

180 Before opening a can of soup, shake can and open bottom end. Soup will slide out easily.

181 Finely grated cheese, added to thin soup, improves the flavor immensely.

182 Unpeeled potatoes add flavor, color and nutrients to stews.

183 Save leftover vegetables in a container in the freezer and use them in soups.

184 To make soup go further, add noodles, macaroni, barley, rice or diced potatoes.

185 To cut meat costs, serve soups, stews, casseroles, etc. with lots of dried peas, beans and lentils.

186 To thicken soup, add one tbsp. (or more) of instant potato.

187 To thicken homemade soup, add a handful of rolled oats or wheat flakes.

188 If your homemade soup is too salty, drop a raw potato in the pot and remove potato before serving.

189 Fat on the top of soup or stew can be removed easily by dropping three or four ice cubes in the pot. The fat will stick to the ice cubes and the cubes can then be scooped out.

190 Take the grease off soup or gravy by swishing a lettuce leaf gently and slowly over the surface. The lettuce will absorb the grease.

FOOD

FOOD

191 Pour leftover soup into ice cube trays and freeze. Remove cubes and store in plastic bags. To use, just thaw as many cubes as needed.

192 Instead of expensive smoked salmon, substitute canned salmon mixed with freshly ground pepper and a squeeze of lemon juice.

193 When using canned shrimp, prechill and they will hold their shape and texture better. Always rinse well in cold water before using.

194 It's easier to skin a frozen fish than a fresh one, so you might find it convenient to freeze fresh fish before skinning.

195 Thaw frozen fish in milk and it will taste like fresh fish.

196 Use up all those broken crackers by rolling with a rolling pin and using the crumbs for coating fish and chops.

197 Add lemon juice to shortening when frying fish. This eliminates smoke and odor.

198 After cooking fish, wash the pan with vinegar to remove fishy odor.

199 To keep lard from splattering while frying, sprinkle in a little salt.

200 Spray your barbecue grill with vegetable oil before barbecuing to make cleanup easier.

201 After cleaning your wok, dry and spray with vegetable oil. This prevents rust.

202 Consider the cost per serving, not per pound, when buying meat. A boneless cut may be cheapest.

203 Separate bacon slices easily by heating the package in the microwave, on high, for 25-30 seconds.

204 Bacon slices will separate smoothly if you slip a pizza cutter between them.

205 Place a large sheet of tinfoil on a baking sheet. Cover it with bacon strips and broil for approximately 10 minutes. This saves cooking and cleanup time since you just throw the foil away.

206 Sausage will shrink less and not break open if boiled about five minutes before frying.

207 Prevent sausage from bursting open and spattering, by piercing the skins with a fork before and during cooking.

208 If you find ham too salty, bake partially, then drain off juices, pour a small bottle of ginger ale over ham and bake until done.

209 To tenderize meat, place in vinegar water for a few minutes.

210 To tenderize steak, rub steak with mixture of vinegar and oil. Allow to stand two hours.

211 To tenderize steak, brush it on both sides with lime juice, a few hours before the steak is cooked.

212 Add a little strong tea to roasts and stews. It acts as a meat tenderizer and reduces cooking time.

213 Tenderize a tough piece of pot roast with tomatoes. Add the tomatoes to the usual vegetables and seasonings and the acid in the tomatoes will act as tenderizer.

214 Buy cheaper cuts of meat and tenderize with inexpensive wine for a gourmet flavor.

FOOD

FOOD

215   Let boiled meat go cold in its own broth if you want it to be tender when cold.

216   Beef liver will be tender if soaked in milk. Refrigerate for about two hours then bread and sauté.

217   Instead of greasing your skillet with oil, sprinkle it with salt lightly and hamburgers will fry in their own juices.

218   To stretch ground beef, mix 1½ cups of poultry dressing with one pound of ground beef. It adds flavor to meat loaf or hamburgers.

219   You can decrease the cooking time for hamburgers by making several holes in the centre of each patty.

220   Brown meatballs uniformly and with less mess by doing them on a cookie sheet in a 425°F oven.

221   Use soybeans instead of hamburger for making meatloaf.

222   If meatloaf is placed on a slice of bacon while baking, it won't stick to the pan.

223   Try making meatloaf in muffin tins. It cooks more quickly and looks better.

224   The trick to cutting meat for Chinese dishes is to partially freeze the meat (or partially thaw frozen meat) and then slice it thinly across the grain.

225 When making a beef stew or gravy, add one tbsp. black-strap molasses for color and flavor.

226 If the gravy gives out before the roast does, don't use expensive gravy mixes. Instead, use instant beef or chicken bouillon to stretch beef, chicken and turkey gravy. Add a teaspoon or two of the bouillon to a tumbler of water; add flour or cornstarch then mix with a fork and add what's left of the gravy.

227 Cutting your own chicken pieces and chops from whole fryers and loins will easily save 30 to 50 per cent on your meat bill.

228 Defrost chicken by soaking in heavily salted cold water. The meat will be white and flavorful.

229 To make baked chicken easier and tastier, brush chicken pieces with mayonnaise, then coat with crushed, seasoned cracker crumbs and bake. The mayonnaise provides an excellent base and the crumbs stick better.

230 When stuffing a large turkey, line the cavity with cheesecloth, then stuff it. After the turkey is cooked, the stuffing is easy to get out and nothing is left clinging to the bones.

231 Use dental floss to truss turkey or chicken.

232 Save one-third the baking time, by placing chicken or turkey in a well-oiled brown paper bag. Seal end of bag with staples and bake in 400°F oven.

233 Baste turkey with a mixture of two cups water and ¼ cup honey.

234 Don't throw away chicken and turkey livers, hearts and gizzards. Simmer them in water, then cut up. Place water and cut up pieces in blender. Blend and add to gravy.

235 For easier carving, cover a roast or turkey with tinfoil and let stand for about 30 minutes after cooking.

FOOD

236 To enable you to have slow-cooking porridge oats in the morning, measure oats into a thermos flask the evening before. Pour on appropriate amount of boiling water and put on lid. Porridge is hot and ready to eat for breakfast.

237 Buy plain cereals rather than the 'with fruit and nuts' variety. Add a handful of raisins, dried chopped apple, prunes, apricots, walnut chips, etc. to make a less costly mixture.

238 To keep dumplings light, prick them open when first taken from the kettle.

239 For light pancakes and waffles, replace the liquid in the batter with club soda.

240 Crêpes can be made ahead of time, frozen in meal-size amounts and reheated in the microwave.

241 If you have pancakes left over, line each with wax paper so they don't stick, place in plastic bag and freeze. When needed, pop into toaster.

242 If you have leftover eggnog, substitute it for the milk called for in plain muffin recipes. It's also good in pancakes.

243 You won't need to invest in a lot of muffin tins if you arrange sealer bands on a cookie sheet then place paper muffin cups in each band.

244   When making cupcakes or muffins, use an ice cream scoop to get the right amount of batter in each muffin cup.

245   If you have trouble getting muffins out the pan, place the bottom of the hot pan on a wet towel for about 30 seconds.

246   If you freeze baker's yeast, it will last indefinitely.

247   Store an opened bag of flour in an air-tight container or plastic bag to maintain moisture content.

248   Whole-wheat flour stays fresh in a freezer bag in the freezer.

249   When baking buns or bread, place rising dough in oven with light on — temperature is perfect and area is free of drafts.

250   Cut fresh bread with a hot knife.

251   Warm hot dog buns in top of double boiler, while wieners cook in the bottom.

252   Stale rolls can be revived if you spray them lightly with cold water, place in a paper bag or wrap in foil and warm in a 375°F oven for about five minutes.

253   Reheat stale buns and rolls by placing them in a wet brown paper bag and putting it in the oven at 350°F for seven to ten minutes.

254   Don't throw away a stale loaf of bread. Wrap it in a damp cloth for about a minute, then place in preheated 350°F oven for about 20 minutes. Serve warm.

255   Save all leftover bread trimmings and crusts. Put them in a plastic bag and freeze. When you have accumulated enough, use for making bread crumbs, croûtons or stuffings.

256   To freshen dry bread, rolls or doughnuts, place in a covered casserole and place casserole in pan of hot water. Heat thoroughly in the oven.

FOOD

FOOD

257 Make your own croûtons. Butter both sides of two or three slices of bread, season as desired and cut into small cubes. Set cubes on cookie sheet and heat them in a 375°F oven for about 15 minutes or until lightly browned.

258 If you run out of bread crumbs, you can use dry cereals by putting them through a blender or food processor.

259 To make bread crumbs, place pieces of dry bread into a plastic bag and roll with a rolling pin.

260 Make up bread crumbs ahead of time and store for months in plastic bag or container in the freezer.

261 Keep crackers in the sugar canister to keep sugar from caking.

262 To deter mold, wash your bread box with a mixture of two tbsp. vinegar to a quart of water.

263 You can easily determine whether you need a fresh supply of baking powder by pouring ¼ cup of hot tap water over ½ tsp. of baking powder. If the mixture doesn't bubble actively, it's too old.

264 To store brown sugar, wrap it in a plastic bag and place in a coffee can which has a snap-on lid.

265 Brown sugar will keep soft if stored in the freezer.

266 Soften brown sugar by freezing it. It will be soft when thawed.

267 To moisten brown sugar which has hardened, place apple slices in a container with the sugar and cover tightly.

268 Brown sugar can be softened by enclosing a slice of bread in the bag. It will be soft in approximately a day.

269 To soften hard brown sugar, place in sealed container with a couple of marshmallows.

270 One cup of white sugar and two tbsp. molasses make one cup of brown sugar.

271 For a brown sugar substitute, mix together ½ cup white sugar, ½ tsp. maple flavoring and ½ tsp. molasses.

272 If you do not have any squares of chocolate for baking, substitute 3 tbsp. cocoa plus 2 tsp. shortening for each square. It's just as good and so much cheaper.

273 When making cookies, add one tsp. of jam or jelly. The cookies will have a better taste and will stay moist longer.

274 To make cakes, cookies, pancakes and waffles especially moist, add two tbsp. honey to the batter.

275 Always store coconut in airtight containers or sealed plastic bags to prevent drying out.

276 For tinted coconut, add a few drops of food coloring to a small amount of water. Pour over flaked or shredded coconut in a jar. Cover and shake until thoroughly colored.

277 One tsp. of cornstarch will improve texture and flavor of fudge.

278 A little flour added to icing sugar makes it go a lot further.

279 Marshmallows will not dry out if stored in the freezer. Cut up with scissors when you want to use them.

280 When cutting marshmallows or gumdrops, dip scissors in hot water.

FOOD

FOOD

281 Crushed cornflakes can be used as a substitute for pecans.

282 Coarse bran may be used in place of chopped nuts when making chocolate brownies.

283 Keep nuts, especially Brazil nuts, in the freezer. They will come out of the shell easier and won't break up.

284 Walnuts which have an 'old' taste can be improved in flavor by pouring boiling water over them, then spreading in a shallow pan and heating in the oven. Stir often to prevent burning.

285 Keep peanut butter fresh by storing the jar upside down.

286 When you double a recipe, just use the original amount of salt.

287 For a quick and inexpensive ice cream sauce, melt one Fudgesicle for two servings.

288 To color sugar for decorating cakes, cookies, etc., put one or two drops of food coloring in a small plastic bag. Add one or two tsp. of white sugar and tie top of bag securely. Work sugar and coloring together with fingers until sugar is evenly colored.

289 A small two-inch paintbrush will last longer and stay more pliable than a pastry brush.

290 Rinse your measuring cup with oil, then rinse in hot water, before measuring sticky liquids. They will pour easily.

291 To make cake flour, sift together two tbsp. cornstarch to one cup of all-purpose flour.

292 When making quick breads, cakes and cookies, cut sugar by one-third to one-half. Bring out sweetness by using vanilla extract.

293 Creaming shortening and sugar is easier if a few drops of water are sprinkled on top of the mixture.

294 When making a cake, always add two tbsp. boiling water to the butter and sugar mixture. This makes a fine-textured cake.

295 When making a cake, or any recipe that calls for mixing dry ingredients together then adding them at a later point, put them all in a paper bag or plastic bag and shake to mix. You have no separate bowl to clean and no fuss or muss either.

296 If batter always rises up the mixer beaters, spray the beaters with a nonstick vegetable oil spray before using.

297 Roll raisins or dried fruit in flour before stirring them into cake batter to prevent them from sinking to the bottom.

298 To keep raisins from sinking to the bottom of your cake, toss in butter or heat in oven for a moment before stirring into batter.

299 Leave cloves out of spice cake if you plan to freeze it. Cloves get stronger in cold storage.

300 Keep a mixture of equal parts flour and shortening at room temperature. Use to grease cake pans.

301 Line cake pans with margarine wrappers instead of wax paper.

302 Use the parchment from margarine and butter wrappers to grease cake and cookie pans.

303 Quick-cool angel food cake by inverting pan over a tray of ice cubes.

FOOD

304 Sprinkle cake plate with granulated sugar to prevent cake from sticking when serving.

305 To keep icing from running off a cake, dust the cake with powdered sugar before icing.

306 When you're ready to frost the cupcakes you've made to pack in lunches, don't frost the tops. Slit the cupcakes in half, frost the centres and put back together. This way, the frosting won't stick to the sandwich bags.

307 Use a clean squeeze-type ketchup or mustard container for decorating cakes.

308 Make a handy, disposable paper funnel for icing cakes by snipping off a corner of an envelope.

309 Before placing a tube cake in a cake server, put a glass or plastic bottle with water in the centre of the cake. This will keep the cake extra moist for a week or longer.

310 A slice of apple or potato under the cake plate dome will keep cake fresh.

311 When you are slicing only a few pieces from a freshly-baked cake, take the slices from the centre then slide the two halves together. The cake will stay fresh longer.

312 Attach a slice of bread, with toothpicks, to cut edge of a cake. This will keep cake fresh until it is cut again.

313 Slice leftover cake, wrap individual pieces and freeze. Put in school or work lunches and the cake will be thawed by noon.

314 Don't throw away stale cake — you can make a fine dessert with it. Soak pieces of the cake in rum, then mix into a thick vanilla pudding and chill. Cover with whipped cream or decorate with slivered almonds or serve with fruit syrup.

315 If you're running low on flour, substitute fine bread crumbs, plain or toasted, for all or part of the flour in cookies.

316 Cookie dough that is to be rolled is much easier to handle after it has been chilled 10 to 30 minutes. This keeps the dough from sticking, even though it may be soft.

317 Sliced cookies from refrigerator dough will always be perfectly shaped if you freeze the dough in small frozen juice cans or plastic wrap cartons.

318 When rolling out dough on wax paper, aluminum foil or plastic wrap, wet the surface of the counter before smoothing the paper down and the water will keep the paper in place.

319 Don't ruin a pan of cookies. Always bake one cookie first, even when using a familiar recipe, because the moisture content of flour can vary greatly.

320 When sprinkling sugar on cookies, use a salt shaker or empty spice container.

321 Save meat trays and freeze muffins, cookies, portions or slices of cake on them. They can be stacked neatly in the freezer without crushing or crumbling.

322 For better pie crusts, make certain all ingredients are cold and do not overwork the dough. Cover the dough and refrigerate before rolling out.

323 To roll out pastry, use two squares of wax paper which have been lightly floured. Roll out the pie crust dough between these sheets. When the pie crust is the correct size, peel off the top sheet of wax paper; invert over the pie plate and peel off the bottom layer of paper.

FOOD

FOOD

324 Keep a small plastic bag handy while making pie crust, kneading bread or mixing meat loaf. Use it to slip your hand into if you have to answer the phone, doorbell or open the refrigerator or cupboard door.

325 Pastry will be flakier if you include one tbsp. orange or lemon juice as part of the liquid.

326 To prevent a pie shell from blistering, place a few slices of bread in it before baking. Remove bread during the last few minutes of baking time. The bread can be used for croûtons in soup.

327 To prevent the bottom pie crust from becoming soggy, grease pie plate with butter before putting in dough. The crust will be soft and flaky.

328 Sprinkle sugar on pie crust before adding cream filling. This will prevent a soggy crust.

329 Minute Tapioca is excellent for thickening fruit pies — two tbsp. for a small pie and three tbsp. for a larger, deeper fruit pie.

330 Short pieces of drinking straws inserted into the centre of a pie will stop the juices from escaping or running over in your oven.

331 Place a layer of marshmallows in the bottom of pumpkin pie. The marshmallows will rise to the top, forming a fluffy topping.

332 Meringue will not shrink if spread on pie so that the meringue touches all edges of the pie crust.

333 Always bake a two-crust pie on the bottom shelf of the oven. This will bake the bottom thoroughly and the pie will brown lightly on top.

334 For fluffy meringue, add ¼ tsp. white vinegar to three egg whites.

335 To keep the edge of a pie crust from getting too brown or burnt, cut out the centre of a foil pan to the exact size of the pie that you are baking and place it over the pie just as soon as it begins to darken.

336 To remove chiffon pie from pie plate with graham cracker crust intact, dip pan in warm water for a few seconds.

337 Use a buttered knife to slice soft pies easily.

338 Store popping corn in the freezer and use it directly from the freezer. You will get puffier, larger kernels of popcorn and more of the kernels will pop.

339 Keep popping corn in the refrigerator and you will get fewer unpopped kernels.

340 Preheat the hot-air popcorn popper and you will have very few unpopped kernels and fluffier popcorn.

341 Instead of buying baby food, purchase frozen vegetables and purée them in your food processor. Spoon into ice cube trays and freeze. Wrap in individual servings for future use. The same process can be followed for daily leftovers of meats and vegetables.

342 Make your own baby food and freeze it in disposable bottle liners. Measure the food into the sac inside the bottle, twist-tie it and slip it out the bottom of the bottle. Increase amounts of food in the sac as baby's appetite increases. It's a sanitary way of freezing baby food and it doesn't take on any freezer odors. To use, just dip sac in warm water, slide food out and heat.

FOOD

LAUNDRY

343 Soak new, brightly colored garments in cold, salty water before laundering. The colors will stay brighter.

344 When washing colored or printed material for the first time, add one tsp. Epsom salts to one gallon of water. The material will neither fade nor run.

345 Soaking blue jeans in ½ cup vinegar and two quarts water for one hour before the first washing helps prevent them from fading.

346 When washing blue jeans, wash in cold water, put in dryer for 10 minutes or so, then fold on a wooden clothes hanger and continue to dry.

347 Always turn corduroy pants inside out before washing. This will keep them lint free and they will also last longer.

348 Pin socks in pairs before washing them and you won't waste time trying to match them up.

349 Rub a sticky zipper with a lead pencil.

350 Rub beeswax inside and outside your zippers on boots, purses, jackets, etc. to keep them running smoothly and quietly. This also removes dust and grime.

351 To save on drycleaning bills, wash your wool blankets in a mild dishwasher soap or Zero on a gentle cycle. Dry on air fluff.

352 Silk garments must be hand washed. Use cool water with Lux or Zero soap. When rinsing, add a bit of lanolin to restore and protect the material. Drip dry and press, using a soft cloth.

353 Club soda is a great stain remover for clothing.

354 To make your own spot remover, combine two parts water with one part rubbing alcohol.

355 Glass cleaner is a good spot remover. If you get a spot on a dress, for example, place a tissue on your hand under the spot. Give the spot a spray of glass cleaner and rub gently, using another tissue on top to make the spot disappear. Reapply if necessary.

356 To make your own prewash spray combine ⅓ cup each of water, liquid detergent and ammonia. Mix, then store in a spray bottle. This is excellent to spray on collars, spots and stains.

357 Use vinegar to remove perspiration, grass and slight scorch stains from clothing.

358 To remove stains, soak garment in baking soda and water for several hours, then wash as usual.

359 Dissolve your soap flakes thoroughly in water before putting into washing machine. This will eliminate powdery buildups on clothes and extra washings.

360 To use up slivers of soap, put them in a white sock, tie a knot in the sock and toss into the washing machine. This will keep your socks whiter and save money because you add less detergent.

361 Always measure any detergent used with appropriate scoops. This prevents using an excessive amount.

362 If you accidentally put too much soap in the washer, pour two tbsp. vinegar or a capful of fabric softener into the machine.

LAUNDRY

LAUNDRY

363 To make certain that clothes receive a thorough rinsing, add one cup white vinegar to the rinse cycle. This will help dissolve the alkalines in soaps and detergents, plus it will give you soft, sweet-smelling clothes.

364 When washing clothes, use cold water for the rinse cycle. Clothes will retain their shape and color better.

365 Clean your washing machine by occasionally running through the wash cycle, using warm water and vinegar. Do not put clothes in for this.

366 For a whiter wash, add ¼ cup dishwasher detergent to your load of white wash.

367 Dishwasher detergent can be used to whiten sweat socks and cottons. Just add to regular washload.

368 Instead of bleach, use about three tbsp. peroxide in your wash.

369 White socks can be white again if you soak them in boiling water to which a slice of lemon has been added. Wash as usual.

370 To bleach handkerchiefs, soak ½ hour in sour milk and wash as usual.

371 To whiten lace, wash in sour milk.

372 To remove blood stains, cover stains with a paste of meat tenderizer and cold water, let stand 15-30 minutes, then sponge with cool water.

373 To remove blood stains, dab with hydrogen peroxide. It will fizz up and the stain will disappear.

374 To remove blood stains from clothing, sponge the stain with three-percent hydrogen peroxide. Let soak for a few seconds, rub, then launder as usual.

375 When fruit juice is spilled on a tablecloth or clothing, boil a kettle full of water and pour full kettle directly over the stain. The stain will be removed immediately.

376 Scrub toothpaste into grass stains for removal.

377 To remove grass stains from children's clothing and white shoes, just rub the stain well with molasses, leave overnight, then wash with soap (not detergent.) The stains will disappear like magic.

378 Most grass stains can be removed with methyl alcohol. (REMEMBER: Test colors first to see if they are affected.) If a stain remains on white material, use a mild solution of sodium perborate, chlorine bleach or hydrogen peroxide.

379 Grease and oil stains may be removed from fabric by first rubbing lard on the spots, then wash with liquid detergent. Repeat if necessary.

380 Put ¼ cup Spic and Span in your wash water for each tub of clothes to help remove stains and grease.

381 To remove grease and dirt spots, put cornstarch on grease spots and rub in. Brush off the cornstarch.

382 Greasy work clothes will wash easily if you add a bottle of cola to the detergent.

383 To remove grease or lipstick stains, pour Mr. Clean on the stain, rub in and wash normally.

384 To remove lipstick from linen napkins, dab on a little petroleum jelly, then wash.

LAUNDRY

LAUNDRY

385 Place clothing, which has gum stuck to it, in the freezer for a couple of hours. Remove from freezer and crumble off gum.

386 To remove ink from clothing, use a dab of toothpaste.

387 Ink stains on clothes disappear when hairspray is used on them prior to washing the article as usual.

388 To remove ink from any material, place a slice of raw tomato on the ink spot. It will soak up the ink and then you can wash the material as usual.

389 To remove ballpoint pen from dolls, use a lemon juice and salt mixture on the ink and leave in the sun for a few hours. Wipe clean.

390 Wet iodine stains with water, then put baking soda on thickly and let stand.

391 To remove ring around the collar, rub shampoo on the ring and wash in the usual manner.

392 For ring around the collar use a mixture of ⅓ cup Palmolive dish soap, ⅓ cup ammonia and ⅓ cup water. Place mixture in a squeeze bottle and rub on with an old toothbrush.

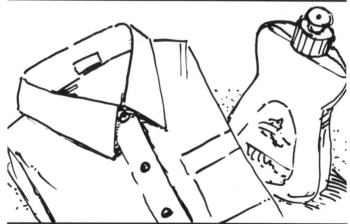

393 Buy a large bottle of liquid starch concentrate and mix one-part starch to one-part water and pour into a spray bottle to make your own spray starch. A light spray of starch helps prevent ring around the collar and protects against various stains.

394 To remove rust marks from clothing, squeeze lemon juice on the spots, pat with salt and hang the garment in the sun to dry.

395 To remove tar from clothing, rub tar with lots of butter and scrub until the tar is removed. Use Spray & Wash or similar product to remove the butter.

396 To get rid of tea stains from a tablecloth, dab with glycerine, leave overnight and then wash in normal manner.

397 To remove candle wax, melt wax between blotters or rub with ice cubes and scrape off. Wax dye stains can be removed with alcohol or bleach in water.

398 Place water-stained fabric (curtains for example) in salted water and soak until the stain disappears.

399 To remove red wine from a tablecloth, moisten spot, apply salt, let stand a moment or two and wash thoroughly as usual.

400 To remove smoke odor from clothing, fill the bathtub with hot water to which a cup or two of vinegar has been added. Hang articles of smoky clothing in the bathroom overnight, keeping the door closed. The vinegar will neutralize the smoke odor.

401 Put a drop of Nilodor in each load of laundry to eliminate all odors.

402 To remove mildew from shower curtains, wash in a mixture of ½ cup bleach, one gallon water and ½ cup detergent.

403 When washing plastic curtains or tablecloths, add one cup vinegar to the rinse water. The plastic will dry soft and pliable thus prolonging the life of the item.

404 To soften stiff plastic pants and prolong their use, put them in a dryer wih a load of towels.

405 To keep your sheer curtains wrinkle free, add a package of unflavored gelatin, which has been dissolved in a cup of boiling water, to the final rinse.

LAUNDRY

LAUNDRY

406 When washing drapes and wanting that perfect pleated effect, press, hang, open and run fingers down each individual pleat, while holding together at the bottom. Wrap a tie around the centre and about two-thirds of the way down. Leave for 24 hours.

407 Use rubbing alcohol to remove ballpoint pen marks on clothing and upholstery.

408 If your slipcovers are washable, place back on your furniture while still damp. They will fit better and won't require ironing because as they finish drying they conform to the shape of the furniture and stretch out the wrinkles.

409 Rubbing cornmeal into a grease stain on upholstery and vacuuming it the next day will lift out the mark.

410 Spruce up old stuffed nonwashable toys by placing in a bag with baking soda. Shake and brush off.

411 Clean white kid gloves with flour. Just rub it into the dirt and brush it away.

412 To clean silk flowers, put flowers in a plastic bag with a couple tablespoons of salt. Shake vigorously while holding stems and bag shut. The dust will cling to the salt and the flowers will look like new.

413 Dry lingerie on a clothes line or place on a clothers hanger to dry. Heat from the dryer will ruin the elastic.

414 Use half of a fabric-softening sheet for a regular-size load of laundry in the dryer. It is as effective as a full sheet.

415 Mix two cups fabric softener with two cups water and store in covered plastic container. Dip an old facecloth in the solution and use instead of fabric softener sheet.

416 Lint from the dryer and from the washing machine, along with other garbage collected in the laundry area, can easily be placed in the empty soap box. This saves space in the garbage and also saves on garbage bags.

417 To remove burrs from sweaters or slacks, use disposable razors.

418 For best results when hand washing sweaters, put a capful of hair cream rinse in the final rinse.

419 Wool is weak when wet. Do not pull, wring or rub wet wool garments. Lay the garment on a towel, roll it up and gently squeeze.

420 Shrunken woollens may loosen and stretch if soaked in a hair cream rinse.

421 To unshrink woollens, dissolve one oz. Borax in one tsp. hot water and add to one gallon warm water. Immerse garment, pull gently into shape and rinse in one gallon warm water to which two tbsp. vinegar have been added.

422 To tighten stretched sweater cuffs, dip in hot water and dry with a hairdryer.

423 Turn acrylic sweaters inside out when washing them to avoid getting fuzz balls on them.

424 To avoid ironing clothes, take them out of the dryer as soon as it stops and fold them.

425 If you can't iron damp clothes right away, put them in a plastic bag and place in the freezer. They will be easier to iron and there's no danger of mildew.

426 To keep delicate fabrics from becoming shiny when ironing, cover the material with a sheet of tissue paper. Make certain the iron isn't too hot.

LAUNDRY

LAUNDRY

427 An iron heats faster than it cools. Therefore, iron fabrics which need a cool temperature setting first, then iron fabrics which require higher temperatures.

428 Pressing pleats in a skirt will take less time if bobby pins are used to hold them in place. They may be left in position while pressing all but the hem and then removed to complete the job.

429 Place a sheet of aluminum foil under your ironing board cover. It will hold the heat longer.

430 Scorch marks may be removed by using a cloth dampened with vinegar. Place it over the scorched area and apply a warm iron.

431 To treat scorch marks on cotton, press with a warm iron on a cloth dipped in peroxide.

432 Stop your iron from sticking by running it back and forth, while hot, over a piece of paper on which salt has been sprinkled.

433 When your iron is off and unplugged, use pipecleaners dipped in sudsy water to clean out the steam holes.

434 Clean a dirty iron bottom with a dampened SOS pad. Then, warm the iron and run over a piece of wax paper to restore the shiny finish.

435 Before you wear a new garment (or even on old ones) touch the centre of each button, front and back, with clear nail polish. This will seal the threads and the buttons will stay on much longer.

436 Find buttons easily. Sort them by size or color in the compartments of an egg carton.

437 When sewing on a button, especially a large one, place a pin under the thread at the back of the button. When finished pull out the pin. The button has room to move and will last longer.

438 Sew buttons on children's clothing with dental floss — it's much stronger than thread.

439 When removing buttons from a discarded item, sew them together before storing with your spares. It will save you the time of having to match buttons later.

440 Button popped off? For a quick fix, reattach it with the wire from a twist tie.

441 Stop tangled thread. For a single thread, knot and cut from spool last; and for double thread, knot each end separately.

442 Wet your finger before slipping on your sewing thimble. The suction will keep the thimble from slipping off.

443 Always place a used desk blotter under your sewing machine needle when oiling the machine to keep from soiling thread and material.

444 To sharpen your sewing machine needle, stitch through a piece of fine sandpaper.

445 When elastic that is sewed on a garment becomes worn or stretched, just baste cord elastic through the worn elastic. Pull it up and knot.

446 When patching the knees of your gardening jeans, leave the top of each patch open like a pocket so that you can slip in pieces of foam rubber for knee pads. They will make kneeling more comfortable.

LAUNDRY

LAUNDRY

447 Save old drapery draw cord and use the good portions for replacement drawstrings in rugby pants and pyjamas. Just thread through the waistband, using a large safety pin, and make a knot in each end to hold.

448 Discarded neckties make interesting women's belts when three are braided together. Single ties may be opened to serve as a neck kerchief on a dress or sweater.

449 Men's cotton-blend shirts make good coveralls or aprons. Just cut away the collar, shorten the sleeves (if long sleeved) and finish the neckline with bias tape.

450 When the feet on men's socks wear out, cut them off at the ankle. Stitch along the bottom and use as children's socks.

451 Using your old quilted housecoat for the inside of a baby quilt makes use of a useless housecoat and is an inexpensive light filling for the quilt.

452 To recycle wrinkled ribbon, run through a warm curling iron.

453 To wear sheets evenly, place a safety pin in the bottom end of your sheet. After every wash, place the safety pin to the other end of the sheet and make your bed with that end to the bottom.

454 When a bedsheet begins to show wear, cut the sheet in half across, bring the unhemmed top and bottom ends together and sew them together. Hem the centre ends with one narrow hem and one wider hem. The worn ends will be on the top and bottom of the sheet, making the sheet last a few years longer.

455 Recyle old bedsheets by cutting them into pillowcases.

456 Cotton sheets can be recycled into pillowcases.

457 Old flannel sheets can be used to make a child's nightgown or pyjamas.

458 Trim old tablecloths into a number of napkins.

459 Turn two old bath towels into a duvet cover for your cat's bed. Simply sew together on three sides like a pillow slip and slide in a scrap piece of fibreglass insulation batting, wrapped in a plastic drycleaner's bag. The cover is easy to slide off for laundering.

460 Baby's receiving blankets can be sewn together to make a special quilt.

461 Key chains sewed into the collars of children's coats and jackets provide strong hangers.

462 When small children have difficulty zipping their jackets, make it easier for them by attaching a key ring to the zipper pull.

463 To make a child's 'emergency throw-away apron,' take a plastic shopping bag with hand holes at the top and cut down one side and across the bottom. Open and use as an apron by pinning at the back.

464 To remove scuff marks from white shoes, rub with dressmaker's chalk and polish.

465 Give suede shoes a new look by wiping with a sponge moistened in cool black coffee.

LAUNDRY

LAUNDRY

466 A cloth dampened with vinegar will remove grease stains on suede shoes.

467 Add extra shine to your shoes by putting a couple drops of lemon juice on them when polishing.

468 Furniture polish is an excellent substitute for shoe polish. Spray an even coat on the shoes, wipe dry and buff to a shine.

469 Polish your shoes well once, then when they look dull wipe them with a soft cloth dampened with baby oil.

470 Paint heels of shoes with clear nail polish to prevent scuffing the finish.

471 Spray the insides of new running shoes with spray starch and let dry overnight. The starch will keep the insides clean and keep the runners fresher for longer.

472 After washing running shoes, spray with spray starch. This will help resist soil.

473 To dry the inside of children's winter boots or summer rubbers quickly, put the hose of the vacuum cleaner into the boot and turn on the blower.

474 To make children's shoelaces last longer, stitch up and down new laces with the sewing machine before putting in shoes.

475 If your shoelaces are always coming undone, dampen with a spray of water before tying.

476 To renew shoelaces which have lost their plastic tips, dip the ends in nail polish.

477 If sandals pinch, dab the inside with rubbing alcohol and wear them immediately. The leather strap will ease a bit over the tight spot.

478 Kerosene will soften boots and shoes which have become hardened by water.

479 Erase 'wet' rings on smooth leather boots by brushing spots with a mixture of equal parts vinegar and cold water.

LAUNDRY

GROOMING

480 Here's an inexpensive bath oil: use peanut oil, safflower oil or sunflower oil in a hot tub of water. Put your favorite herbs, lavender, basil or rose petals in a little bag and let the water run over it. You get the oil and the sweet scent for little cost.

481 To save on bubble bath, make your own by placing your soap slivers into a terry drawstring bag. Dangle bag from the tap at bath time, allowing the water to run over and through it.

482 If you run an inch of cold water in the bathtub before adding hot water, your bathroom will be free of steam.

483 To save on hand soap, stock up when it's on sale, then unwrap each bar before storing. This allows the bars to dry out and become harder, which makes them last longer when used.

484 To make your own liquid hand soap, you need one (3.5 ounce) bar of soap (choose soap which contains moisturizing cream) and three cups of water. Grate soap, add water and microwave on high until well dissolved. Stir every two minutes. Cool and pour into a dispenser.

485 To use up small pieces of soap, soften in the microwave for a few seconds on a piece of plastic wrap. Then add to your new bar.

486 Bits and pieces of hand soap can be used up by putting into a toe of a nylon stocking and tied.

487 After washing and drying your hands, make a cup of one hand and pour in some vinegar. Carefully coat both hands as you would with hand cream. You will have soft hands.

488 Rub your hands with vinegar to get rid of food odors such as fish, garlic and onion.

489 Vinegar will remove fruit and vegetable stains from hands.

490 To get the onion smell out of your hands, rub them with a little dry mustard.

491 To remove paint smells from your hands, use water and lemon juice.

492 Dip hands in lemon juice to whiten fingernail tips.

493 Before going to work in your garden, rub your nails over a bar of soap. This will prevent the dirt from getting your nails.

494 Lather soap in your hands and add ½ tsp. sugar to the lather to remove gardening stains from your hands.

495 To save money on special soap, use laundry detergent as a hand cleaner for greasy, oily hands.

496 If you're bothered by hangnails, place Vitamin E around the cuticles.

497 Baby oil does the same job as cleansing creams but at less than half the price.

498 To save on costly facials here are two inexpensive homemade treatments. For normal to oily skin: one cup yogurt, one tsp. fresh lemon juice, one tsp. fresh orange juice and one tsp. carrot juice. Blend ingredients and apply to face, leaving on 10-15 minutes. Rinse with tepid water. For dry skin: ¼ mashed avocado, ½ mashed banana, two tbsp. plain yogurt and one tsp. wheat-germ oil. Combine and use as directed above.

499 Use solid canned shortening as a makeup remover.

GROOMING

GROOMING

500 Blemishes will fade if you dab a little lemon juice on them.

501 Lemon rubbed on the skin will keep it white.

502 At the end of the day, lemon slices rubbed on the feet will freshen them

503 Dead skin will peel off elbows, knees, feet and face which has been massaged with Miracle Whip Salad Dressing.

504 For an inexpensive shampoo, mix ½ cup vinegar, ½ cup dish detergent, ¼ cup water and two tsps. mayonnaise.

505 To stretch shampoo, mix one pouch of unflavored Knox gelatin into one cup of warm water. Shake well. Pour your shampoo into a quart jar and add gelatin mixture.

506 Make every drop of shampoo count. To use those last drops in the bottle, add a little water, shake the bottle and use. This works for hair conditioner as well.

507 Put an end to shampoo waste by filling a clean plastic pump bottle with shampoo. A few pumps will deliver the desired amount of shampoo and there will be no more spills.

508 To add lustre to brunette or red hair, after shampooing rinse with black coffee, followed by clear water.

509 A bit of vinegar in the final rinse water will make hair shiny.

510 If your young daughter's hair has a tendency to spring out of rollers, fold strips of wet-strength facial tissue around each strand of hair before rolling on the roller. The curls will dry quickly and will be softer.

511 To remove gum from a child's hair, apply Spray & Wash generously to the gum then rub hair between fingers. Comb the gum out and wash hair.

512 To remove gum from a child's hair, use a little peanut butter and rub until the gum disappears.

513 For an inexpensive homemade deodorant, make a dusting powder of equal parts baking soda, cornstarch and a pinch of ground cloves.

514 Use baking powder as a deodorant. Just pat it on as you would powder.

515 Clean dentures with lemon juice for a fresh-tasting mouth.

516 Soak your dentures in white vinegar overnight. It's an inexpensive and effective way to clean them.

517 TV commercials show toothpaste applied the full-length of the brush. All that is necessary is about ¼ inch on the brush.

518 If you run out of toothpaste, use baking soda.

519 Get the last bit of toothpaste out by placing the tube under hot water before rolling and squeezing it.

520 To get rid of onion breath, chew parsley with vinegar on it.

521 Another way to get rid of onion breath is to drink a cup of strong coffee.

522 Use a little salt in warm water for a mouthwash.

523 Put your dentures in a cup of bleach for about 10 minutes. Rinse thoroughly and your dentures will be sparkling clean.

GROOMING

GROOMING

524 If you use a razor and foam to shave, dry your blades well after use and apply a thin layer of petroleum jelly. Then, with a soft facial tissue, wipe off any excess jelly. This will form a coating over the blades, making them last up to five times longer and ensuring a comfortable shave the next morning.

525 To make your own hand lotion combine four ounces glycerine, two ounces alcohol, one dram gum-tragocanth (chips) and one pint of warm soft water. Mix and let stand 24 hours, shaking often. A favorite perfume could also be added.

526 Make your own suntan oil cheaply by combining ½ cup olive oil and ½ cup cider vinegar.

527 Fill a jar of pressed rose petals (or any sweetly-scented flowers), add as much glycerin as the container will hold and cover tightly. After three weeks or so, pour off the perfume into a perfume bottle.

528 If you're getting tired of your perfume and want to switch for awhile, put your old bottle in the refrigerator. It will not deteriorate and you can go back to it again when you feel like it.

529 Don't throw away perfume that is not "you" — use a few drops in the bathtub or sprinkle a few drops on a lightbulb for a lovely scent when the light is turned on.

530 Store nail polishes in the refrigerator. They will go on more smoothly and last much longer.

531 Grease the threaders on nail polish bottles and the lids won't stick.

532 Brushes and combs will come out like new if you soak them 15-20 minutes in a pot of lukewarm water to which one tbsp. baking soda or a little ammonia has been added.

533 To clean hairbrushes, after hair has been removed, rinse brushes throughly in cold water to which ammonia has been added. Shake and dry.

534 To clean hairbrushes and combs combine ¼ cup bleach, one cup water and two tbsp. baking soda. Put in a jar and let combs and brushes soak in solution for a few hours. The solution can be reused. (CAUTION: This solution will break down protein (hair) and therefore, cannot be used to clean natural fibres such as pig bristle.)

535 Contact lenses lost? Turn out the lights and use a flashlight. The lens will show up when the light falls on it.

536 Use pierced earrings as a brooch on a sweater. That way they serve a dual purpose.

537 Put a piece of chalk in your jewelry box to prevent costume jewelry from tarnishing.

538 To prevent tangled necklaces, hang from cup hooks which have been put into a wooden hanger.

539 Use fishing line to restring necklaces. It's easy to handle and extremely strong.

540 Use empty egg cartons to store jewelry — the bottom for earrings, the lid for necklaces.

541 When a ring gets stuck on your finger due to swelling, place your hand in a bowl of ice water. Soak until the ring slips off.

GROOMING

FIRST AID

542 For an inexpensive antacid powder, use ½ tsp. baking soda in a glass of water.

543 When a pill sticks in your throat, eat a banana. The soft bulk of the fruit moves the medication along.

544 To get a young child to take distasteful medicine, run an ice cube over his tongue — this temporarily freezes the tastebuds.

545 For a cough remedy try this. Boil a lemon in a cup of water. Remove lemon, cut in half and extract juice. To the juice add ½ cup honey and mix well. Take a teaspoon at a time as needed. Stir well before taking each dose.

546 To get relief from a sore throat, gargle with one tsp. salt in ¾ cup warm water.

547 Putting a dab of honey on the back on your tongue can bring relief from a nagging cough.

548 Use Watkins oil and black pepper on the forehead and sinus area for quick headache relief.

549 Hot coffee burned your tongue? A few grains of sugar sprinkled on the sore spot will undo the misery.

550 Soothe a minor kitchen burn by rubbing it gently with the cut surface of a raw potato.

551 When cooking and you get a burn from a grease splatter, spray immediately with hairspray. It seals off the air and takes away the sting.

552 Ease a burn from hot grease with vanilla extract.

553 A bit of toothpaste on a small burn is a quick healer.

554 To treat minor burns, keep an aloe vera plant in the kitchen. Break off part of the fleshy leaf and split it open. Apply to the burned area.

555 For burn or sunburn relief, apply cold iced tea. Dip a sponge in the tea and pat gently on the burn every 10-15 minutes until the pain is relieved.

556 Put vinegar on sunburns and they won't blister.

557 For sunburn, mix some salt into ice cold milk. Sponge the sunburn once or twice with this mixture.

558 Put Epsom salts in your bath water to relieve aches and pains.

559 To get relief from wasp stings, soak stung area in ice water, to which a little Dettol has been added.

560 If you are stung by a bee, head to the spice rack — ¼ tsp. meat tenderizer added to one or two tsp. water (enough to make a paste) will stop the pain in seconds.

561 To relieve itching from mosquito bites, apply a bit of toothpaste.

562 To get rid of hair lice, boil quassia chips (obtained from any herbalist) into a tea. Wash hair with this tea and rinse well.

563 For rashes or chicken pox, make a paste of cornstarch, baby oil and a small amount of water. Pat on the paste to stop the itch.

564 Sprinkle cornstarch, instead of powder, on baby's bottom after washing and drying. This will help prevent diaper rash.

FIRST AID

FIRST AID

565 To take the sting out of removing adhesive bandages, saturate the area with baby oil before pulling off bandages.

566 Clean a child's scrape with a red washcloth so the blood won't show.

567 Apply ice to a splinter before removing. It eliminates the fussing.

568 If you hit your thumb or finger accidentally with a hammer, immerse in cold water immediately. This will ease the pain and helps to prevent swelling.

569 To help prevent varicose veins, elevate your legs for 20 minutes each day.

570 If you need a hot water bottle in a hurry, fill a plastic two-litre soft drink bottle with hot water, screw on top and wrap in a towel.

GENERAL CLEANING

571 To make your own all-purpose cleaner combine ¼ cup baking soda, one cup household ammonia, ½ cup white vinegar and one gallon warm water. Mix in a large pail and use as needed. Store in clean Javex containers or other plastic jugs. Label with felt pen. Use at room temperature.

572 Put your liquid cleaner (Mr. Clean etc.) in a spray bottle. It makes wipe-ups quick and easy and saves on the amount of liquid you use.

573 When doing general household cleaning, use a small toothbrush to clean small cracks.

574 If your sponge mop is starting to shred, wrap a sock over it.

575 Clamp old socks into a holder to make a great dry mop.

576 Cut the best parts of worn-out towels into squares and use as dishcloths and dusters.

577 Use old socks, underwear, T-shirts etc. for cleaning rags.

578 Make your own window and glass cleaner. Combine ½ cup household ammonia, two cups of 70 per cent isopropyl rubbing alcohol, one tsp. liquid dish detergent and add water to make one gallon. Store in an ice cream pail with lid and transfer to spray bottle as needed. (NOTE: Poison, keep away from children.)

579 One part vinegar and three parts water makes an excellent window cleaner.

580 For a perfect window washing solution, add ½ cup ammonia, ½ cup white vinegar and two tbsp. cornstarch to a bucket of warm water.

581 Make your own window and appliance cleaner by adding two tbsp. of vinegar, two to three drops of liquid dish detergent and blue food coloring to two quarts of water.

582 Never wash windows on a sunny day. They will dry too fast and streak.

583 When washing windows during cool weather, wet your cloth with automobile windshield washer solution. Wipe windows and dry with paper towels.

GENERAL CLEANING

584 And for another window cleaner — dilute windshield washer fluid one-to-five with water, add one tbsp. vinegar and pour into spray bottle.

585 For cleaning large windows and patio doors get a bottle of rubbing alcohol and add a tsp. or two of straight ammonia. Mix and put in an empty sprayer bottle. This mixture cuts dirt and will not streak.

586 Use a little starch in the water to wash mirrors. It removes soil and gives a polish to the glass.

587 To make woodwork, windows and mirrors sparkle, clean with cold tea.

588 Place the crystals from your chandelier in a pillow case, fasten case securely and place in rack in dishwasher. They come out sparkling.

589 To dry clear decanters, use a hairblower or put over a heat register.

590 Clean flower vases with a solution of one tbsp. salt and one cup vinegar. Soak overnight.

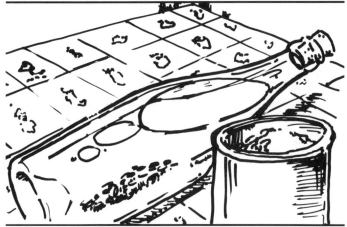

591 Clean narrow-necked bottles by using a vinegar and water solution. Add some dry rice to produce a scouring effect when bottle is shaken.

592 Use toilet bowl cleaner to remove mineral deposits on glass bottles.

593 Round typewriter erasers are excellent for removing paint spatters from window panes.

594 Scratches on glassware will disappear if polished with toothpaste.

595 Tiny chips can be taken out of fine crystal by rubbing the chipped edge with a fine silicon carbide paper (No. 320 grit).

596 A small nick in the rim of a glass can be smoothed with an emery board.

597 To remove price-tag glue, rub with a paper towel and a dab of peanut butter. The oil in the peanut butter cleans the glue off glass or plastic and leaves no stain.

598 Use vegetable oil to remove sticky tags from glass, ornaments or brass. It leaves no trace of glue.

599 To remove fingerprints from photos, spray with hairspray and use soft cloth to buff.

600 For an inexpensive diamond cleaner, dip diamonds in full-strength vinegar, rinse with clear water and polish with a soft cloth.

601 To clean gold jewelry, use a solution of half ammonia and half water with a dash of liquid soap. Let jewelry soak in the solution for a few minutes and then take a soft toothbrush and clean around any etchings or stones. Rinse well and polish with a soft cloth. (DO NOT use on pearls or any soft stone.)

602 Dry-clean costume jewelry by placing in baking soda and brushing lightly.

603 When storing silver for an indefinite period, wrap a small piece of camphor with it to prevent tarnishing.

604 Stored silverware won't tarnish if you tuck a small piece of alum into your silver chest.

605 To clean small silver items, rub a small amount of toothpaste over them with a damp cloth and rinse clean.

GENERAL CLEANING

GENERAL CLEANING

606 To shine silver flatware, place in an enamel pan lined with aluminum foil, cover with boiling water, add three tbsp. baking soda and let stand for a few minutes. Rinse and dry. This method is not recommended for pieces with cemented-on handles or for silver with a carved or raised design, accented by a dark finish.

607 To clean brass, combine ¼ cup salt with enough vinegar to dissolve. Add flour to make a paste.

608 Polish brass with Worcestershire sauce and then brighten by rubbing with olive oil after each polishing.

609 A lemon peel dipped in salt will clean tarnished brass.

610 If brass isn't overly tarnished, wash it in water in which potatoes have been boiled.

611 To clean brass or copper, use a soft cloth and some ketchup. Clean off with a damp cloth and rub to polish.

612 To clean copper and brass, wash thoroughly then dip a soft cloth in vinegar and then in whiting or salt and scour the metal. Wash and dry, then rub with a soft cloth.

613 For an inexpensive copper cleaner mix together one tbsp. flour, one tbsp. salt and one tbsp. vinegar.

614 Mix together one-part salt to five-parts vinegar and pour into used detergent bottle. Use for cleaning copper.

615 Instead of using copper cleaner, you can clean copper-bottomed pots and other kitchen utensils with toothpaste and a damp cloth.

616 Use used fabric softener sheets for dusting. They pick up all lint and dust and leave furniture clean.

617 To make your own dustcloths, put hot sudsy water into a large jar with two tsp. of turpentine. Shake jar and put some old rags inside. Let sit overnight, then wring out and hang to dry. These rags will clean off the dust and leave furniture shining.

618 A carwash glove serves as a perpetual furniture duster. Impregnated with polish, it will serve over and over before needing washing.

619 Keep an elastic band around your bottle of furniture polish to hold your cleaning cloth.

620 Keep an automobile brush with your household cleaning things. It's great for dusting underneath sofas, chairs, appliances and other hard-to-get-at corners.

621 For those popular, but high maintenance venetian blinds, rub a fabric softener sheet over the slats and it will repel the dust that so quickly seems to accumulate on them.

622 Cheesecloth over the heat registers cuts down on dust.

623 To remove pet hair from furniture and pillows, dampen a sponge with a solution of warm water and glycerin or just use water. Squeeze the sponge thoroughly and lightly brush over furniture.

624 Homemade furniture polish: ½ cup vinegar, one cup boiled linseed oil, one cup turpentine, ¼ cup methylated spirits. Mix vinegar and oil gradually to a thick cream; then add turpentine and spirits. Bottle and shake well before using.

625 Put ordinary Vaseline on a soft cloth and apply and polish as you would furniture polish. The Vaseline soaks into the wood and restores dried-out furniture. It also brings out the grain and leaves a lasting natural lustre.

626 Glycerin or olive oil on your dust rag removes dust easily and leaves items polished.

627 Baby oil makes ideal furniture polish, at less than half the cost of commercial polish.

628 For an inexpensive furniture polish, combine equal quantities of boiled flaxseed oil, white vinegar and turpentine. Shake together.

629 Wet glasses, hot dishes, alcohol and perfume will leave white marks on wooden furniture. To remove the marks and restore the original color, use a solution of two parts alcohol, two parts turpentine and one part olive oil and rub it in well with a cloth.

630 To remove white heat marks on furniture, apply a thin paste of salad oil and salt. Let stand one to two hours, wipe off and polish.

631 To remove water marks from furniture, mix cigarette ashes with a little Vaseline and rub on spot.

632 Water stains on a table can be removed with paste of cigarette ashes and butter or margarine. Rub with the grain of the wood.

633 To remove scratches in furniture, rub a peanut over the scratches.

634 Darken a small scratch in varnished wood with a walnut or pecan. The flaw almost disappears.

635 Cover scratches on brown or cherry mahogany with old iodine which has turned brown. For red mahogany, use new iodine and for maple, try diluting iodine with denatured alcohol, half and half.

636 For burns on a wood table, swab the burn with nail polish remover, then gently scrape away with a dull knife until the burn is gone. Fill the indentation with layers of clear nail polish, then cover with regular furniture polish.

637 To remove stains from woodwork, put furniture oil on a cloth, then dab on a little baking soda and rub on the stain.

638 To clean wood panelling, remove any old furniture polish with Varsol or other petroleum solvent and a clean cloth. Buff with a dry cloth to remove streaks. From then on, just use a damp cloth or sponge and a drop or two of dish detergent to clean the panelling when necessary. Always buff with a dry cloth after cleaning.

639 To remove two-faced tape without damaging the wallboard, spray well with petroleum-based prewash spray and ease off with blunt-edged knife or spatula.

640 To whiten piano keys, wash with rubbing alcohol.

641 To prevent pottery from scratching the furniture, use some self-stick bunion pads on the bottoms of the pottery.

642 To prevent chairs scratching the floors, put self-stick bunion pads on the bottom of the chair legs.

643 Wax chair leg bottoms to prevent scratching the floor when chair is moved.

644 If an egg falls and breaks on the floor, sprinkle the egg generously with salt and let stand a short time. Then wipe up with a cloth or paper towel. It comes up clean and leaves no mess on the floor.

645 Before using a cloth to wax the floor, soak it in cold water and wring out. You will find that the cloth will not absorb the wax and you will save a good deal of wax which otherwise would have been wasted.

GENERAL CLEANING

GENERAL CLEANING

646 Instead of using commercial preparations, you can wax a floor by washing it with one gallon warm water to which two tbsp. furniture polish and ½ cup vinegar have been added. Unused portion can be bottled for future use.

647 Use liquid wax on rubber or vinyl mats.

648 When cleaning floors which have been waxed, put a small amount of vinegar in cold water. Wash floors with this. The cold water won't remove the wax and the vinegar will remove the dirt. It works and the floor retains its original shine.

649 Use ammonia to remove floor wax.

650 Before sweeping away broken glass, wet the end the broom. It will pick up small scattered pieces of glass which you can't see.

651 Put a coat of wax on your dustpan. Dust and dirt will slide off easily.

652 Remove tar from vinyl floor by rubbing it with butter or margarine. Wipe with a dry cloth.

653 Save old hairbrushes and use them to clean your vacuum, lint trap on your dryer or to dust behind radiators.

654 Before you dust or vacuum, tape a small paper bag to your apron or belt so you can drop in stray pins, crayons, etc. which you find along the way.

655 Reuse your vacuum bags by carefully slitting open the bottom with a razor blade or sharp scissors and emptying the bag. Then seal shut carefully with tape.

656 To vacuum Christmas tree needles, put a pantihose leg on the nozzle. The vacuum will draw up the hose as well as the needles so you will have to hold the pantihose around the nozzle. When you are finished, just pull out pantihose and throw away. No need to worry about a plugged up vacuum hose.

657 Give carpets a liberal sprinkling of salt before vacuuming. It helps destroy moth larvae and brightens colors.

658 To get mud out of the carpet, sprinkle with cornstarch, let stand 15 minutes, then vacuum.

659 Most spots on carpet can be eliminated by rubbing a slice of white bread over the area, then vacuuming. The bread should be one or two days old.

660 For grease stains on carpet, sprinkle cornmeal on area, brush lightly, leave overnight and then vacuum.

661 Use shaving cream as a spot remover for cleaning carpets. Wash it out with water or club soda.

662 To remove most stains from your carpet, sprinkle with salt and sponge out.

663 To remove fresh spills and pet stains from carpet, blot spill with paper towel, saturate with soda water, let sit for five minutes and blot with paper towel. The stain will be gone.

664 Instead of using expensive brand-name carpet deodorizing products, sprinkle baking soda on the carpet, wait 10-15 minutes, then vacuum. The baking soda absorbs pet and smoke odors and leaves a fresh smell.

665 To get rid of pet odors on carpets, use a spray bottle containing white vinegar and spray the area.

666 To prevent static shock from carpeting, mix one-part liquid fabric softener with five-parts water in a spray bottle. Mist the carpet lightly.

GENERAL CLEANING

GENERAL CLEANING

667 When you want to move furniture in a carpeted room, but hesitate because of indents caused by the furniture, place a damp cloth on the indentation and place an iron (on low setting) on top of the cloth. Hold just long enough to heat. This will relift the carpet fibres and then simply brush the fibres to their original position.

668 Here's an easy way to wash walls. To one gallon of warm water, add two tbsp. baking soda, four oz. vinegar and four oz. ammonia. Use a sponge and wash from the bottom of the wall up to the ceiling to prevent streaks. You do not have to rinse.

669 A cloth dampened with turpentine will remove crayon marks from painted walls or wallpaper.

670 Crayon marks can be removed from painted walls by rubbing them with a cloth dampened with lighter fluid.

671 Crayon can be removed from walls by coating the mark with toothpaste and letting it set for approximately 15 minutes before wiping clean with a dry cloth.

672 Black marks on walls can be removed with a soft, damp cloth and some toothpaste.

673 To remove grease spots on wallpaper, make a paste of cornstarch and water, let it remain on the spot until dry, then brush off.

674 To clean nonwashable wallpaper, rub gently with an art gum eraser or a crustless piece of bread.

675 Windowsills are easy to clean if you give them a coat of wax. Wax protects the paint and dirt wipes off in a jiffy.

676 You can scent the house by simmering cloves and cinnamon on the stove. It also adds humidity. The same spices can be used over and over again for this purpose.

677 Dab a cottonball in wintergreen oil and hide somewhere in the room. The room will stay fresh for months.

678 A small container of vinegar left in any room of the house keeps the room smelling fresh even when the house is closed up for a while.

679 Add vinegar occasionally to the water in your humidifier. It will keep the air fresher.

680 An inexpensive and quick method of freshening up your home is to apply vanilla extract to a cloth and wipe on lights in various rooms throughout the house. A fresh, clean aroma is released when you turn on the lights.

681 To remove smoke from a room, dip a towel in equal parts vinegar and water. Wring out and whirl gently over your head.

682 To stop butts burning in the ashtray, line the bottom with one inch of baking soda.

683 To rid tap water of chlorine smell, fill a pitcher and let water stand overnight.

684 To ensure a pleasant, clean smell from your garburator (garbage disposal), grind lemon rinds or add a few drops of lemon juice after you turn off the garburator.

685 New paint odor can be disposed of by placing a large plate filled with salt in the room.

686 Drains and toilet bowls can be deodorized and sanitized with vinegar.

GENERAL CLEANING

GENERAL CLEANING

687 Put a few drops of vanilla in a small glass and place in the refrigerator to banish food odors.

688 Baking powder placed in the refrigerator and freezer takes away odors and keeps the refrigerator fresh.

689 A teaspoon of lemon extract in your cleaning water will eliminate bad smells in your refrigerator.

690 To deodorize refrigerator, cut a raw potato in half and place inside the refrigerator, cut side up. Just pare off when it turns black.

691 The least expensive refrigerator deodorizer is two charcoal briquettes.

692 Place a piece of barbecue charcoal inside the freezer to eliminate stale freezer odors.

693 If a plastic storage container has an unpleasant smell, fill it with water, add a few drops of vanilla extract and let stand overnight.

694 To remove damp and musty odors in closets, place used coffee grounds in an open container in the closet. This can also be used to the refrigerator to control odors.

695 Clean mildewed surfaces with a rag soaked in fresh lemon juice and salt.

696 Remove mildew from a leather suitcase by wiping it down with a cloth moistened in a solution of equal parts rubbing alcohol and water. Dry in an airy room.

697 Clean sliding door gliders, then run either parafin wax or a candle over them to facilitate easier, quieter opening and closing.

698 Clean your telephone with rubbing alcohol to keep it looking new.

699 To clean a soft rubber eraser which has become soiled from use, rub it against an ink eraser. This cleaning action works both ways as the soft eraser will remove smudges from the harder, more abrasive ink eraser.

GENERAL CLEANING

KITCHEN CLEANING

700 When liquid dish detergent container appears empty, add small amount of water to it and you'll have enough for a few more washes.

701 Add a bit of vinegar to your dishwater. This will cut the grease, allowing you to use a cheaper brand of detergent.

702 Put one tbsp. of bleach in your water when washing dishes. It kills germs.

703 One tbsp. of bleach in the dishwater will keep the dishcloth clean and smelling fresh.

704 Use hot water for washing dishes, but make certain you wear rubber gloves.

705 Use baking soda to clean Corning-type dishes.

706 Brighten discolored enamel ware with a paste of salt and vinegar.

707 If you have burned food on the bottom of a cooking pan, let sit overnight with vinegar and Comet covering the burned area. It wipes out easily the next day.

708 To give burned food the brush off, let a mixture of half water and half vinegar soak in the pan overnight. The burned food comes off easily the next day with a light scouring.

709 When you scorch a pan, try sprinkling dry baking soda over the scorch. Let stand awhile and clean as usual.

710 To remove burned-on food stuck to enamel saucepans, place a strong salt solution in the pot and let soak several hours. Cover the pot, place it on the stove and bring solution to a slow boil. This usually removes the burned food safely.

711 A few drops of bleach in lukewarm water will remove tea stains from cups and teapot.

712 A paste of baking soda and water will remove coffee and tea stains from porcelain and china.

713 To clean a coffee pot, use one denture tablet in cold water and soak overnight.

714 To remove coffee film from thermos bottle, pour in one tbsp. raw rice and one cup of warm water. Shake well and rinse.

715 To remove brown grease marks from pots, chrome burner rings, etc., soak in ammonia overnight.

716 To remove rust from baking pans, dip a raw potato in any cleaning powder, then scour the pans.

717 Rust can be removed from a knife blade by plunging it into an onion and leaving it there for an hour or so. Work blade back and forth a few times and wash in soap and water.

718 To remove food stuck to a casserole dish, fill with boiling water and add two tbsp. baking soda or salt.

719 When purchasing meat wrapped in plastic mesh, save the mesh. Wrap the mesh in a ball, secure with a plastic garbage bag tie and use as a pot scrubber.

720 To preserve plastic pot scrubbers, place them in plastic mesh grape bags. Twist and slip the mesh bag back to double it and tie a knot in the end. The pot scrubbers will last twice as long.

721 A small ball of tinfoil works well to clean your pans inside and out.

KITCHEN CLEANING

722 Keep a toothbrush in your kitchen. It's great for cleaning small areas such as beaters and graters.

723 Steel wool soap pads won't rust if you keep them in the freezer or refrigerator.

724 Cut an SOS pad into four pieces. It lasts much longer because using the whole pad causes it to rust before the next use.

725 Fill soap cups in dishwasher only half-full. This saves on dishwashing soap and your glasses will not get water marked and scarred.

726 Use equal amounts of dishwasher soap and baking soda in your dishwasher. Your dishes and silver will be cleaner and so will the machine.

727 To remove scum from glassware, add ½ cup bleach to wash cycle in dishwasher and ½ cup vinegar to the rinse. The vinegar neutralizes the bleach.

728 If your dishwasher or dishes become stained from hard water, just run a package of Tang orange juice crystals through the dishwasher with the stained dishes in it.

729 If your dishwasher needs cleaning, use powdered laundry bleach instead of dishwasher detergent in an empty machine. This will clean and disinfect the dishwasher.

730 To remove lime buildups in your dishwasher, put ¾ cup laundry bleach into empty dishwasher and run it through first wash. After this drains, add two cups vinegar and run through the rinse cycle, but not the drying cycle. Reset the dishwasher for a full cycle, using dish detergent.

731 If the inside of your dishwasher is discolored due to iron deposits, run washer through a cycle using ¼ cup of Oxalic Acid Crystals (can be purchased at the drugstore). Then run through a second cycle with just water.

732 When water discharges from a portable dishwasher into the sink, a fine spray splashes over the sink and sometimes onto the floor. To prevent this, cut out the bottom of a quart-size milk carton and slip this on the discharge pipe of the dishwasher. The water will flow directly through the carton into the drain.

733 When using the automatic dishwasher, open the door and turn the cycle to off when the washing cycle has finished and let the dishes air dry.

734 For a sparkling white kitchen sink, place paper towels across the bottom of your sink and saturate with household bleach. Let sit for at least a half hour.

735 For fragrant, clean sinks, pour ½ cup baking soda, followed by one cup vinegar, down the drain. Let bubble 15 minutes, then rinse with warm water.

736 Instead of expensive cleaners, use baking soda to clean your stainless steel sink.

737 Club soda can be used to shine a stainless steel sink.

738 To remove alkali corrosion around taps, etc., use straight vinegar.

739 Kitchen taps can be kept free of water spots if you polish them with a coat of liquid wax.

740 Stainless steel sinks may be brightened by using a cloth dampened with vinegar.

741 To get rid of rust marks on stainless steel sinks, rub with lighter fluid.

KITCHEN CLEANING

742 Clean rusty sink stains by using cream of tartar and a few drops of hydrogen peroxide.

743 A cloth dampened with vinegar will remove rust stains caused by leaky faucets.

744 Place a marble in your tea kettle to prevent the kettle from scaling.

745 White vinegar works well as a scale remover for electric kettles and steam irons.

746 To clean inside of teapot, if scales gather in the pot or spout, pour 1½ to two tbsp. of Spic and Span into empty pot. Fill to brim with boiling water, let stand until cool and rinse well.

747 Run a piece of paper towel through the cutting mechanism of your electric can opener. It will absorb the grease and grime.

748 A damp cloth dipped in cigarette ash will clean the bottom of your electric frying pan.

749 Nail polish remover will take off any plastic which has melted onto the toaster.

750 Dry baking soda and a damp cloth will remove stains from chrome appliances.

751 Use baking soda to clean chrome and the glass door of oven.

752 Sprinkle soda generously on the bottom of your oven, let sit for one hour and wipe clean.

753 If your oven isn't too dirty, a saucer full of household ammonia placed in the oven the night before cleaning will soften the residue. (BEWARE of the vapors when cleaning.)

754 To clean oven racks, put in bathtub with ½ cup dishwasher detergent. Soak for 30-45 minutes. No scrubbing required.

755 To easily clean a broiler pan, sprinkle the hot pan heavily with dry laundry detergent. Cover with a dampened paper towel and let sit for a while.

756 To clean oven and barbecue grills, put in bathtub with ammonia and water.

757 Put an open container of ammonia in a plastic garbage bag with your barbecue grill. Set in the sun for a couple of hours. Take out grill and rinse clean.

758 To clean barbecue and oven grills, place in bathtub with dishwasher soap and hot water.

759 To clean your whole stove from top to bottom, put all removable parts from your stove and oven into a large garbage bag and pour in a couple cups of ammonia. Seal the bag with a twist tie and let it sit for several hours or overnight. Rinse clean with warm water.

760 Put tinfoil, shiny side down, on your gas grill. Turn on high for 10 minutes. When cool, remove foil and the grill will be clean.

761 If something catches fire in your oven, sprinkle the fire generously with salt or baking soda. This will stop the flame and smoke immediately.

762 Place wax paper under ice cube trays in the freezer so they won't stick.

763 To clean a stained bread board, sprinkle with salt and rub it all over with the cut side of a lemon.

KITCHEN CLEANING

764 To remove onion smell from breadboard, sprinkle board with baking soda and scrub.

765 Once every six months cover your chopping board with vegetable oil and let stand overnight. Then, wipe off the oil. The board will last indefinitely.

766 To keep wooden salad bowls from drying and cracking, wipe them inside and out with a paper towel soaked with cooking oil. Do this in the evening and in the morning wipe off excess oil. Repeat about once a month.

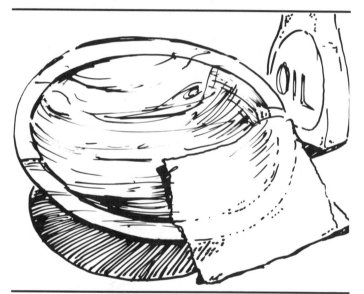

767 To clean counter tops, scrub with a paste of baking soda and water. Let sit for ½ hour and wipe with a wet sponge.

768 Ammonia and water cleans grease from cupboards. Use one-part ammonia to five-parts water.

769 To prevent rust stains under your metal canisters when water is spilled on the counter, keep your canisters sitting on plastic container lids. The lids will raise the canisters about ½ inch off the counter.

770 Keep the top of kitchen cabinets clean. Unroll clear plastic wrap and cover the cupboard top. When cleaning time comes, simply roll up plastic wrap and throw in the garbage. Replace with fresh wrap.

BATHROOM CLE

771 Wipe a little glycerin (available in drug stores) on windows and bathroom mirrors and buff with a soft cloth to keep them from steaming up.

772 For a fast shine to your glass shower doors, wipe them with a sponge containing white vinegar. It cuts soap film quickly.

773 Use baking soda mixed with liquid dish detergent and water to scour the tub and walls and doors of the shower.

774 Clean bathroom tiles with vinegar which has been poured into a spray bottle.

775 One of the easiest ways to clean bathroom walls is to run hot water in the bathtub and shut the door for five minutes. Steam will form on the walls and ceilings and loosen the dirt, which can then be wiped with a dry, clean cloth.

776 The same enzyme presoak that takes stains out of fabric will clean unsightly spots from porcelain sinks. Soak sink and garments at the same time.

777 The rough, grainy texture which forms in bathtubs can be removed by soaking with vinegar.

778 To remove stains from old bathtubs, use a "fine" automotive polishing compound.

779 Use undiluted ammonia to remove bath oil rings from the bathtub.

780 To get rid of mildew stains on sinks, tubs and tiles, pour on bleach, let sit for a few minutes, then rinse.

781 Shine chrome in the bathroom with a cloth dampened with vinegar. Let dry, then polish with a soft cloth.

782 Use hydrogen peroxide in shower door tracks to loosen the hardened scum. When it bubbles up, run a cotton swab along the track and flush with a glass of water.

783 To get the grime and mildew out of shower curtains, fill your washing machine with warm water, add detergent and ½ cup bleach. Let the machine run a few seconds, then put the shower curtains in, along with three or four towels. Let the cycle finish.

BATHROOM CLEANING

BATHROOM CLEANING

784 To get soap film and grime off vinyl shower curtains, spray them down with a vinegar/water solution and then wash them in the washing machine with another cup of vinegar and regular detergent.

785 Use wintergreen oil as a bathroom deodorant. Soak a cotton ball with the oil and place in a glass container. It will last for months.

786 Coat your metal bathroom scales with pastewax to ward off rust from water splashes.

787 Place a denture-cleaning tablet in the toilet bowl and let it dissolve. This is an easy, inexpensive way to help keep the bowl clean.

788 Muratic acid works well for cleaning extra stubborn stains in toilet bowls. (REMEMBER: Caution must be used when using acid.)

789 Put a scoop of Tang in the toilet bowl and let sit for a couple of hours. It eliminates toilet bowl stains, leaving the toilet clean and fresh smelling.

790 Pour leftover cola drinks into your toilet bowl. Let soak, then flush and the bowl will sparkle.

791 Save old toothbrushes for cleaning around difficult areas in the bathroom.

792 A sponge makes a great soap dish.

793 To keep soap from melting in a wet soap dish, put a pop bottle cover on the soap to keep it from touching the surface of the dish.

PANTIHOSE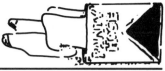

794 Store onions in old pantihose or nylons.

795 Cut a thin strip around a pair of discarded pantihose, stretch and use to sew buttons on coats or children's clothing.

796 To save a lot of work for no extra cost, take a white nylon stocking leg, cut off the foot, boil the hose a few minutes, then dry. Tie one end of the leg and use this bag to hold the bread stuffing for chicken or turkey. When poultry is cooked, the dressing can easily be removed.

797 Wash old pantihose and use as stuffing for stuffed toys (either as replacement stuffing or for use in homemade toys).

798 Spray Static Cling to your pantihose before putting them on. They're easier to pull on and underclothes will not cling.

799 Wear gloves when putting on pantihose and save your pantihose from snags and holes caused by rough or long fingernails.

800 Pantihose will last longer if you freeze them before wearing. Wet, wring dry, place in a plastic bag and put in the freezer. After the pantihose have frozen solid, thaw and hang to dry.

801 Always buy two of your favorite pantihose — same shade and texture. When one leg runs, simply cut it off and save the rest until a leg runs on the second pair. Then, by wearing both pairs, with one leg each, you've created a new pair at no extra cost.

802 Using hairspray on the heels and toes of sandalfoot pantihose will help them last longer.

803 Pantihose and nylons make an excellent filling for quilts or cushions. The quilts and cushions are easy to wash and dry quickly.

804 Use pantihose to strain paint.

805 Add one tsp. of vinegar to the rinse water for pantihose to help them retain their elasticity.

806 Use old pantihose to tie plants to stakes.

PANTIHOSE

PANTIHOSE

807 Save the white cardboards from pantihose and use them for writing grocery lists and notes.

808 If your fan belt snaps, use a pair of pantihose as a substitute. Cut to fit.

809 When you have pantihose with only one good leg, cut off the good leg and save it until you get another of the same color and use them with a garter belt.

810 If you forget to wash out your pantihose ahead of time and need them right away, wash them and place in your hairdryer hood. Turn on dryer and your hose will be dry in minutes.

811 When hanging pantihose outside on the line to dry, put a teaspoon in each foot. They won't blow over the line and get snagged.

ENERGY

812 Make certain that everyone turns off the lights when leaving the room. For extra incentive, charge 25 cents when a person leaves a room without shutting off the lights.

813 A dimmer switch will save on light bills.

814 To save money, reduce the wattage of the bulbs you use.

815 It is more economical to use one large bulb rather than several small ones. A 100-watt bulb gives as much light as six 25-watt bulbs, but uses less than $\frac{2}{3}$ the power.

816 When your night light bulb needs replacing, use a Christmas tree lightbulb — it's the same size.

817 Don't forget the lightbulbs when dusting. A dusty bulb will give off up to 50 per cent less light.

818 To save energy, do not preheat the oven before cooking casseroles or meat dishes.

819 For foods which require a long cooking time, it is more economical to use the oven than a burner on top of the stove.

820 Conserve energy by cooking the entire meal in the oven.

821 When cooking dinner in the oven, cook your canned vegetables by removing the label, taking off the lid and cooking in the tin can in the oven for about 15 minutes.

822 When baking, oven heat can be lowered 25 degrees if you use glass or ceramic baking dishes, which retain heat better than other materials.

823 Do not fill the kettle to the brim before boiling if only a few cups of water are needed. Boil only what you need.

824 Operating the dishwasher only once a day will consume less water and electricity.

825 To save on power, wash bath towels in cold water.

826 Partially dry bath towels in the dryer, then hang on chair backs or a clotheshorse to finish the job. This will save energy and will add humidity to the house.

ENERGY

827 Instead of using the dryer, hang clothes outside to dry. In the winter, set up a clothes line in your basement.

828 Clean the dryer vent after every load to reduce energy use.

829 By purchasing a simple dryer vent control device, you can use the heat from the dryer for your basement or garage.

830 Use a 24-hour timer for your car block heater and interior warmer.

831 Installing a transient voltage surge suppressor at the electrical panel, could save money when using household appliances.

832 Use your bathroom fans sparingly in the winter. The fans remove warm air.

833 Run the furnace fan constantly during cold weather to reduce your heating bill.

834 Keep your furnace well tuned. A slipping belt can reduce the efficiency of your furnace by as much as 50 per cent.

835 Spray the furnace filter with furniture polish to increase the amount of dust it picks up.

836 Be certain your furnace has the proper amount of oxygen for maximum heat from your fuel.

837 Place aluminum foil behind each of your radiators. It will reflect heat back into the room instead of allowing the wall to absorb it.

838 Turn down the thermostat when you go out for the day.

839 Before retiring for the night, turn down your thermostat to 16-17° C (60-65° F).

840 To save fuel costs, install a set-back thermostat so that the temperature is maintained at a lower level while sleeping or when no one is home during the day. The initial investment is paid back in a short time through lower heating bills.

841 Close off heat and doors to unused rooms.

842 Keep your closet doors closed. There is no need to heat or cool them.

843 Cover your basement windows with some inexpensive material for the winter so heat is not lost through the glass and frame.

844 Draw your drapes closed and open only during sunny periods to conserve heat in the winter.

845 In the winter, block off radiators and open drapes on the sunny side of the house. This will keep the rooms on that side of the house warm.

846 On older homes, use plastic inside or outside to cover windows and frames to help cut drafts and cold.

847 Seal your windows in the winter to conserve heat.

848 If you have a milk chute which is not in use, pack it with fibreglass insulation to prevent drafts and frost buildup.

849 White foam meat trays can be washed, cut to size and fitted under wall switches etc. to prevent drafts.

850 Remove baseboards and caulk crack between wall and floor to prevent drafts along outside walls.

851 Make certain that your house is properly insulated and all air drafts plugged to prevent heat loss in the winter.

ENERGY

ENERGY

852 To help stop heat loss from the foundation of your house during the winter, shovel three or four feet of snow up against the side of the house to act as insulation.

853 Insulating the outside walls of your basement will pay for itself after three winters.

854 Keep blinds pulled down and drapes closed in the summer to keep the house cool and cut down on air conditioner use.

855 Keep your hot water heater in the mid range.

856 Turning down your hot water heater several degrees can save you a great deal of money over a year and it could also save you from scalds.

857 If you have to run the water forever until it gets hot, wrap your hot water pipes in an easy-to-apply foam blanket, available at hardware or building supply stores. Not only will you save on the water bill, but your hot water heating costs will be reduced too.

858 Adjust the float on your toilet so that you use less water when flushing.

859 Set a liner inside your toilet tank to conserve water.

860 Turn your water valves on and off every six months to keep them in working order. A stuck valve can cause a flood.

861 Have a timer near the telephone in order to limit long-distance phone bills. Set the timer for a predetermined length and stick to it.

PLANTS

862   Cut flowers from the garden in late evening or early morning. Use sharp shears and take water to the garden and plunge flowers in at once. Cut stems under water on the diagonal so they will not take in air but will absorb moisture well.

863   A solution of two tbsp. vinegar and three tsp. sugar to a quart of water will help cut flowers last longer.

864   Cut flowers will last longer if you keep them in equal parts of water and 7-Up with ½ tsp. of chlorine bleach added to each quart of this solution.

865   To keep fresh cut flowers lasting longer, add a few drops of chlorine bleach to the water, which will also stay fresh and odorless.

866   Drop a copper penny in the water with tulips so they will stand erect and not open wide.

867   To keep cut roses and woody-stemmed flowers lasting almost twice as long, cut the stems diagonally and pound the ends of the stems with a mallet.

868   Put a piece of charcoal in the water and cut flowers won't develop a bad odor when the stems begin to rot.

869   Homemade plant food: To one gallon of water (preferably rainwater or melted snow) add one tbsp. household ammonia, one tbsp. baking powder, one tbsp. saltpeter, one tbsp. druggist sulfur, two tbsp. Epsom salts, one rusty nail (or one Femiron tablet) and two tbsp. liquid soap. Use once a month to perk up your plants. For acid-loving plants add five tbsp. black coffee or four drops of white vinegar to the above recipe.

870   For plants which require acid soil, you may add a few drops of lemon juice or leftover tea water once a week.

871   To ensure that your house plants get enough nitrogen, water once a month with a solution of one seven-gram envelope of gelatin dissolved in one quart of water.

872   Sulphate of ammonia — one ounce to two gallons of water — prepared the evening before watering, is an excellent fertilizer for verbenas and other plants.

PLANTS

873 Save the water from boiling eggs. It is filled with minerals and excellent for your plants.

874 Throw your broken egg shells into a large container and fill with water. Let sit for a week, then discard the egg shells and use the water to feed your plants.

875 A birth control pill dissolved in one quart of water will help ferns grow faster and stronger.

876 Besides regular water, once a month dissolve an Aspirin in a cup of tea and feed to plants.

877 Spider plant, golden pothos or syngonium act as houseplant air cleaners.

878 Weak tea or water with a couple of drops of ammonia and dish soap makes an excellent plant spray. It cleans the plant and keeps pests away.

879 To get rid of indoor plant bugs, put a few drops of liquid detergent in the water when you water your plants. When the bugs go into the soil at night, they should die.

880 A small square of Vapona Strip, placed on the soil of a plant, will quickly get rid of spider mites.

881 Put one tbsp. glycerin in the water for your houseplants. It will make the leaves shine.

882 To brighten leaves on a plant, dip a cottonball in milk and wash each leaf. They will shine better than with costly commercial products.

883 To keep the leaves on your indoor plants looking green and healthy, rub them with castor oil or mineral oil.

884 Wipe plants with a mixture of a little mayonnaise and a little water. You'll have lots of shine and less dust.

885 Never put clay pots directly on wooden furniture because water will seep through the porous clay.

886 Use cottage cheese and yogurt lids for inexpensive plant pot stands.

887 To water your plants (if they are in clay pots which have drainage holes) while you are on holidays, set the plants on bricks in the bathtub and fill tub brick-high with water.

888 If you are going away for about a week, fill the bathtub with about ¼-inch of water. Set each of your plants on a saucer so that the pot doesn't touch the water. Cover the whole tub with a drycleaning bag.

889 If you can't get someone to water your plants while you are away, put all your household plants beside a large bowl of water. Drop ends of yarn into the container of water and then lay the other ends across the stalks of the plants. Capillary action of the water will carry enough moisture to keep the plants fresh.

890 White azalea will last longer than other colors.

891 To have fresh parsley and other spices all winter, plant and grow in flowerpots in the house.

892 Take an old, pithy cooking onion which is sprouting and plant it in a pot. Set in the window or outside and it will continue to grow tops. Just snip off for salads or soups.

893 For inexpensive houseplants, grow your own from avocado pits, orange peels, carrot and pineapple tops.

PLANTS

PLANTS

894 Always use moist soil only for transplanting or repotting to avoid root damage. Moisten soil the day before and dampen peat moss several days before use.

895 Egg shells make a good substitute for pebbles in houseplants. They promote drainage and also add lime to the soil.

896 When repotting plants, place a coffee filter in the pot before filling it with soil. The filter stops the soil from leaking out of the bottom of the pot and making a mess in the saucer.

897 Use chipped or broken cups, bowls, vases or old ornaments for small houseplants.

898 Save empty egg cartons to start your spring seedlings in.

899 You can use old ice cube trays as plant starters. Leaving the sectional part in the tray, press a mixture of soil in each section and plant one or two seeds (depending on kind) in each. Water well. When ready to transplant, gently lift sectional part and each plant will come out easily.

900 Plant seedlings in styrofoam cups. They are economical and the plants are easy to remove when it's time for transplanting.

901 Save empty two-quart milk cartons (cut in half) to use as seed flats when starting garden transplants.

902 Store flower bulbs over the winter in discarded nylon stockings. Hang the bulb-filled stockings in a dry place so the air can circulate through them and prevent the bulbs from molding.

903 Whitewash the inside of your window boxes before filling with earth. This will prevent the boxes from rotting and will help keep away insects.

904 Window boxes won't splatter windows if you put a shallow layer of gravel over the dirt.

905 When transplanting tomato and cucumber plants, put a handful of ashes around each plant. This will stop cutworms, acts as a fertilizer and keeps the soil loose.

906 Before planting onion sets, let them stand 24 hours in a solution of one cup Javex to one quart water. No more maggots.

907 Save garden space by planting radishes in the carrot and lettuce rows. They help mark the slow-germinating carrot row and they help protect lettuce from bugs.

908 If you want to get more out of your vegetable garden, try interplanting. To interplant, you put rows of fast-growing vegetables between rows of slow-growing ones. All the crops are planted at once, but they'll mature at different times. Simply set rows of fast-growing crops such as lettuce, spinach or radishes between slower crops like tomatoes or cucumbers. The speedy ones will be ready for harvest just about the time when the slow ones get large and need the room.

909 Banana skins, placed just below the surface of the soil, rot quickly and supply calcium, magnesium, sulphur, phosphorous, sodium and silica — marvellous for roses and flowers.

910 Save all your egg shells in a plastic bag. Crush with a rolling pin and sprinkle around your rose bushes and flowers. They'll keep the bugs away.

911 Save all your vegetable peels and scraps to make humus or just throw them on the garden in the winter.

PLANTS

PLANTS

912 Cutworm moths seek out mulch and crop residues as egg-laying sites in early spring. Clean up the garden thoroughly every fall and till the soil in early spring to effectively eliminate the larvae.

913 If you have a cutworm problem in your lawn, add three ounces of dish detergent to a two-gallon watering can filled with water. Cover your lawn well, then water in the evening. This will force the cutworms to the surface during the night and they will dry out in the morning sun.

914 Pests or cutworms in the garden? Plant marigold seeds in a border around the garden. This makes a pleasant area and keeps most harmful insects away from your vegetables.

915 Rid outdoor plants of pests by mixing a liberal dose of soap flakes, ¼ tsp. vinegar and approximately four cups water in the plant mister and spraying on affected areas.

916 Prevent worms in your garden onions. Save coffee grounds and let dry. Place at the bottom of each row when planting onions.

917 Tinfoil spread on the ground around plants will keep cats away.

918 Use broken cassette tapes to tie plants to stakes.

919 Water your lawn in the evening to get less evaporation.

920 To kill grass and unwanted weeds growing between cement sections, pour salted, boiling water over them.

921 Vinegar will destroy grass in sidewalk and driveway cracks.

922 Save your old dishcloths and linen tea towels. They make excellent floor rags.

923 Save on paper towels by using old terry tea towels to dry vegetables or for quick mop-ups in the kitchen. Wash and reuse indefinitely.

924 Wax your ashtrays. Ashes will not cling and they can be easily cleaned with facial tissue or paper towel.

925 Nail polish remover will remove gummed labels from ornaments, dishes etc.

926 Hairspray will help remove sticky residue left by price tags.

927 To remove a special label for a coupon offer, wet a paper towel and wrap around the jar, then place the jar inside a plastic bag and twist-tie shut. Let stand overnight and the label will come loose easily.

928 An overload of suds in the sink settles with a sprinkle of salt.

929 Save empty plastic bread bags for storing other foods.

930 To save the numerous plastic bags which come into your home, take an empty cardboard roller from foil or waxpaper and roll the plastic bags onto the roller. They will store neatly in a drawer.

931 Save plastic wrap from meat or bakery goods and roll on an empty paper towel roll. Reuse the wrap as needed.

932 To keep from wasting plastic wrap, because it sticks to the roll and peels off unevenly, put it in the freezer a few minutes before using.

933 Store your plastic wrap in the refrigerator to keep it from sticking to itself.

934 Save all foil or wax paper margarine wrappers from the quarter-pound squares. Then, when making hamburger patties, use an icecream scoop and scoop out hamburger onto each paper. Fold over and pat to desired thickness. Place on cookie sheet and quick freeze, then store in a plastic bag in the freezer.

MISCELLANEOUS

MISCELLANEOUS

935 Thoroughly wash plastic milk pouches when emptied and use for freezer bags. They are much stronger than the bags you buy.

936 Old milk cartons can be filled with water and frozen for use in your picnic hamper.

937 Save money on ice by filling empty vinegar bottles with water, freezing them and placing them in your cooler.

938 Styrofoam egg cartons make great bathtub toys.

939 Save foam egg cartons. They make excellent ice cube trays.

940 If you always find yourself running out of wax paper, save the liners from cereal boxes. They work well.

941 Use wax paper bags from cereal boxes to wrap pies for the freezer. Just slip the pies in and seal with tape.

942 Styrofoam meat trays are handy to have on hand when you take baking etc. to a social function or other event. They come in several sizes and shapes and can be covered with an appropriate serviette to make them more presentable. Wash and rinse them well and store until required.

943 Save plastic containers from cottage cheese, yogurt, margarine etc. and use as containers when freezing food.

944 Wash and save plastic margarine containers for microwave lunches. Throw away or reuse.

945 Use lids of small plastic margarine tubs to separate hamburger patties when freezing. The patties will not stick together.

946 Take the lid from an empty four-litre ice-cream container and cut away the lip. You now have a portable cutting board which can be discarded when it becomes worn.

947 When you can't find a shoehorn, make one out of a gallon plastic container. Just cut to the size you want.

948 Save all plastic food containers and plastic pails. They come in handy around the house when cleaning brushes, mixing glue etc. After the job, they can then be thrown out.

949 Save tin coffee containers with plastic lids. They make ideal freezer containers for muffins and cookies.

950 Label leftovers with a bit of tape on which you can write. Everyone will know at a glance what the containers hold.

951 When saving items in plastic containers, use a wax crayon to label them. To reuse the container, just wipe the writing off with a dry paper towel.

952 Make extras of a favorite meal and freeze TV dinner-style portions. Then, on those nights when everyone is on the run, heat in the oven or microwave for a quick meal.

953 When rubber gloves develop a hole, cut them in strips on the round, both the hand part and fingers, and use as rubber bands.

954 When rubber gloves get a hole in them, cut off the finger portions. They can be pulled over broom and mop handles to avoid handles marking walls.

955 If you always wear out one rubber glove, start saving all the good gloves and by turning half of them inside out you will gain a few extra pairs.

956 Paper towels, used to dry the table after washing it, can be left to dry and used for wiping up messy spills.

957 Always use lunch bags more than once.

MISCELLANEOUS

MISCELLANEOUS

958 When putting curtains, which may fray easily, on a rod which has sharp ends, wrap ends of the rod with scotch tape.

959 Place a small piece of cotton in the fingers of rubber gloves to help prevent holes from fingernails.

960 Sharpen old, dull scissors by cutting through light sandpaper.

961 When pins become difficult to push through a diaper or fabric, push the pin into a bar of soap.

962 A slow cooker can be used as a heater for baby bottles or hot compresses, or it can be filled with soup and plugged in by a patient's sickbed.

963 Put rubber bands around children's drinking glasses to provide better gripping power and therefore cut down on spills and breakage.

964 Place a clean, dry sink mat on the seat of your child's highchair. It will keep him from sliding out of his chair.

965 To make a highchair guard, cut out a section of an old bathtub mat to fit the seat of your child's highchair. The suction cups will adhere to the seat and prevent the child from slipping.

966 Baby's car potty will be much simpler to clean if you line it with a plastic bag and plop the works into a Ziploc bag for disposal at the next stop.

967 Empty facial tissue boxes can be turned upside down and turned into instant garages and houses for bored young-sters to play with.

968 Save large milk cartons and potato chip boxes. Cut off tops and cover with leftover wallpaper to make colorful contain-ers for crayons, markers, games, etc.

969 Cut off the sides and fronts from empty cereal boxes, tissue boxes, dress boxes etc. and save. These clean, firm surfac-es are great for children to use for drawing on. It's much cheaper than buying expensive scrapbooks and drawing paper.

970 Children can make their own greeting cards by cutting out pictures from magazines and pasting on recipe cards. Add a verse and the card is ready to go.

971 Candy Lifesavers make wonderful candleholders for a child's birthday cake. They're colorful, edible and inexpen-sive.

972 For inexpensive stocking stuffers or party treats, glue last year's calendar pictures onto stiff cardboard then cut into pieces for a jig-saw puzzle.

973 For inexpensive gifts, crochet carpets, curtains, coverlets and pillow covers for a child's dollhouse.

974 To make playdough, mix a few drops of food coloring in two cups boiling water. Add ½ cup salt, two tbsp. oil and two tbsp. alum. Knead well and keep in the refrigerator when not in use.

975 For bubble solution for children's bubble pipes use two tbsp. powdered detergent, one tbsp. glycerin, one cup hot water and a few drops of food coloring. Mix well.

976 To remove broken off tips left in the crib board from crib pegs, heat sewing needle on the stove element, pierce cen-tre of broken off tip and pull out.

MISCELLANEOUS

MISCELLANEOUS

977   To restore an old deck of playing cards, dust deck with a small amount of talcum powder.

978   Straighten dented ping pong balls by placing in hot water for 15 minutes.

979   Tired tennis balls can be given new life by wrapping individually in foil and heating for half an hour in the oven at 200°f to restore bounce. They can be reheated several times.

980   For a stocking stuffer make a windowsill bouquet with tiny artificial flowers and a pretty perfume bottle.

981   Here's a stocking stuffer idea. Wrap a bar of colorful, scented soap in nylon netting and tie with ribbon for a fragrant air freshner.

982   Stumped for stocking stuffers? Plan now for Christmas. For the stamp collector, fill a plastic sandwich bag with used postage stamps and a good magnifying glass.

983   Cut up used Christmas cards to make labels for next year's Christmas presents.

984   Instead of store-bought bows for gifts, use pompoms, dried or fabric flowers, measuring spoons, candy canes, balloons, bells, ornaments, barrettes, erasers, combs, etc.

985   Instead of commercial wrapping paper, use wallpaper roll ends. They are stronger and often prettier than wrapping paper.

986 To recycle expensive gift wrap, lightly spritz the wrong side of paper with spray starch, then press with a warm iron.

987 Towels, scarves and fabric napkins make useful wrapping paper.

988 Arrange painted picture frames over newly wallpapered walls for inexpensive, yet effective decorating.

989 Use leftover wallpaper for shelf paper and drawer liners.

990 Save postcards and special occasion cards and laminate them. Use to line shelves and drawers.

991 Squeeze a new roll of toilet tissue before installing. This will prevent waste because it won't roll excessively.

992 Toilet tissue is much cheaper and goes a lot further than facial tissue. Also, you can use more or less as needed.

993 When you receive junk mail which includes return envelopes, use the envelopes to store small items such as seeds, pictures etc.

994 Use the backs of business envelopes and the unwritten side of circulars for writing grocery lists, notes to children, etc.

995 When mailing a get-well card to someone in hospital, use the patient's return address rather than your own. In this way, should the person have been released from hospital, he is assured of getting the card.

996 If your stamps and envelopes are stuck together, place them in the freezer for an hour or so. Then you should be able to spread the stuck part easily with a knife without damaging the glue.

997 The perforated salvage edges on postage stamp sheets make good jar labels for home preserves.

998 If stamps have stuck together, put them in the freezer for a while. They will come apart easily without harming the glue.

999 Dampen the string before tying a parcel. It will not slip and, as it dries, it shrinks and keeps tight.

MISCELLANEOUS

MISCELLANEOUS

1000 To soften the tip of a felt-tipped marking pen which has hardened after being left uncovered for a long time, place a few drops of spot remover in a dish and work the tip around in it. When soft, wipe tip.

1001 To keep track of addresses, use 3x5 cards and make out new ones when addresses change.

1002 To keep addresses handy for your personal correspondence, cut or tear return address label off letters and tape on the back cardboard of your current writing pad. Remove to new pad each time one is started. They are always at your fingertips when writing letters.

1003 Make copies of your credit cards in case they are misplaced or stolen.

1004 When going away on holiday, store important papers in the refrigerator or freezer. In case of fire, the papers will be safe.

1005 When unable to obtain typewriter ribbon to fit your typewriter, save the cans from the old ribbons and rewind it with any available new ribbon.

1006 Make moving day easier for you and the movers. Use colored markers and designate one specific color for each room of the house. The movers will be able to carry your boxes to the correct rooms without needing constant assistance.

1007 Never throw out unwanted "this or that." Place in a box marked garage sale and store until spring. Someone will make you an offer at your next sale.

1008 Form a video rental "co-op" where you have friends over when you rent a video and they have you over when they rent one. Both families save money.

1009 If arthritis is making it difficult to grasp a pen, push the pen through a small rubber ball.

1010 To help an invalid or person of limited mobility, buy a pair of barbecue tongs. They are ideal for retrieving articles which are out of reach.

1011 Instead of buying special trays to give someone breakfast in bed, use a muffin tin. It neatly fits glasses, cups and individual portions of food.

1012 If a screw tends to come out of your eyeglasses, apply clear nail polish over it.

1013 A valuable tool in the kitchen is a nutcracker. It's ideal to use for loosening bottle tops and jar lids.

1014 To open a tightly sealed jar, wrap a rubber tourniquet around lid and it will open easily.

1015 A clothespin makes a great clip for potato chip bags.

1016 When you get a set of measuring spoons, undo the wire holding them together and leave the spoons standing loose in a cup or glass. This way, you need only wash the spoon used instead of the whole set.

1017 Stacked tumblers often stick together and are difficult to separate. To avoid this, drop a toothpick into the bottom of the tumbler before inserting the next one. The toothpick will support the upper tumbler and keep it from sticking in place.

1018 If kitchen glasses are stuck together, fill the top glass with cold water and dip the bottom glass in hot water.

1019 When two glasses or bowls are stuck together, put a few ice cubes in the top one and set the bottom one in hot water. Let stand a few minutes and they'll come apart easily.

MISCELLANEOUS

MISCELLANEOUS

1020 If the plastic pump supplied with commercial window cleaner, hand cream etc. doesn't reach the bottom of the bottle, you can extend the tube with waterproof adhesive tape.

1021 To make old plastic flowers look like new, spray with hairspray.

1022 Soak a new broom in hot, heavily salted water to give it a longer life.

1023 Keep extra shower hooks in sewing basket to hold pins.

1024 Shower hooks can be used as key chains.

1025 Set your alarm clock on a tin plate. It will be heard.

1026 When eating outside, staple the tablecloth at each corner, so the wind can't take it.

1027 When camping, take a roll of clear plastic and a stapler. When the winds blow, just fasten the plastic on trees around the campsite.

1028 Take an old barbecue grill with you when camping. It can be used on any barbecue in any campground and can always be kept clean.

1029 Only grocery shop once a week — you'll save money by buying less.

1030 Never grocery shop on a Monday morning when stock is depleted or anemic.

1031 Always eat before you go grocery shopping. You'll buy less.

1032 Always shop with a grocery list.

1033 Grocery shop alone — leave the kids with a sitter and never take your husband.

1034 Take a calculator when shopping and calculate the cost per unit.

1035 Use manufacturers' coupons, but only for foods which you would normally buy.

1036 Record all expenditures. This slows down spending and people find out exactly where their hard-earned dollars are going.

1037 Check foods on the lowest shelves at the grocery store. They are usually less expensive.

1038 Buy groceries on sale and always buy more than one of the sale items. This way you can stock up on groceries without paying regular price.

1039 Buy as many household items and groceries by the case as possible.

1040 Buy two pairs of the same color socks — when one sock wears out, you always have two more which match.

1041 A candle will fit most candlesticks if dipped in hot water first.

1042 Chill candles in the refrigerator 24 hours before using them. They will burn evenly and won't drip.

1043 Keep two or three candles in the refrigerator freezer. If there is a power failure, they are easy to find.

1044 To prevent a candle from dripping, place a little salt around the top of the candle before lighting.

1045 Crumbled bay leaves, placed in a cupboard, will discourage insects.

MISCELLANEOUS

MISCELLANEOUS

1046 Make your own moth repellent by mixing four oz. of rosemary, four oz. of mint leaves, two oz. of thyme, one tbsp. ground cloves and one tsp. of ground orris root. Let it age for several weeks.

1047 Place cucumber peels on the kitchen windowsill to keep ants out.

1048 Rinse out empty milk carton and use as mini garbage container by the sink.

1049 Use a plastic grocery bag, inserted in a plastic wastebasket to collect garbage under the sink. When the bag is full, use the handles of the grocery bag to tie a firm knot in the bag, then place in your outdoor garbage can.

1050 Keep plastic grocery bags, which are to be used as garbage bags in empty facial tissue boxes. It keeps them tidy.

1051 Used, four-quart milk bags are great for lining the bathroom garbage bin.

1052 To prevent your garbage from filling up so quickly, after emptying a tin can, open the opposite end and flatten the can before throwing away.

1053 To have garbage bags handy, put some of them in garbage pail under the garbage bag in use.

1054 Farm tip: Get paper bags for groceries and recycle as garbage bags. Paper bags help burn the garbage more completely.

1055 Throw a few mothballs into the garbage can to neutralize odors and keep out insects.

1056 Put a few capfuls of Pinesol into bagged garbage to keep cats and dogs away.

1057 Save water from cooked vegetables to mix with your dog's dry food. It will add extra flavor and vitamins.

1058 Attach a rubber suction cup to the bottom of your pet's dish to keep it from sliding while the pet eats.

1059 If your dog knocks over his food dish when eating, anchor a one-gallon pail to the ground by driving spikes through it. If you want to be able to clean it or cut grass around it, buy a tube-cake pan and drop it over a stake driven into the ground.

1060 Store big bags of dry dog food in a clean garbage can with a lid.

1061 Brewer's yeast rubbed on your dog's coat prevents fleas.

1062 Make a portable dog anchor by tying his leash around an old tire and putting a few bricks inside.

1063 If the kids are begging for a dog, have them walk the neighbor's for a month.

MISCELLANEOUS

HANDY PERSON TIPS

1064   Rub petroleum jelly on the hinges and door knobs before you start to paint a door. If you get paint on them, they will wipe off easy.

1065   To keep white paint from yellowing, add 10 drops of black paint to each quart of white.

1066   When painting ceilings, cut a child's rubber ball in half and put your paint brush in one of the halves to catch the drips.

1067   An old pair of swimming goggles will protect your eyes from paint splatters and drips when painting ceilings.

1068   When painting, protect your hands and face with moisturizer. Cleanup will be easier and the moisturizer will prevent paint from seeping into the pores.

1069   To stop paint from dripping, punch a few holes in the rim of the paint can. When the brush is wiped against the edge, the paint flows back into the can. The lid covers the holes so the paint won't dry out.

1070   Before pouring paint from a can, cover the rim with masking tape. After pouring, remove the tape — the rim will be clean and the cover will fit tightly.

1071   To remove lumps from paint: Cut a piece of screen to fit the inside of the paint can. Set it on top of the paint and let it float down to the bottom of the can. It will take all the lumps with it, trapping them at the bottom of the can.

1072 When painting a room, dip a small card into the paint so that you have the exact color with you and can match accessories in stores.

1073 When painting inside corners, trim the paint brush bristles to a V to save strokes and spread paint more evenly.

1074 When you poke a paint brush into corners or allow it to rest on the bottom of the paint can, the bristles curl and stray. To straigthen natural bristles (not synthetics), try wrapping the brush in a couple of thicknesses of damp cloth and press gently with an iron. The steam and cloth binding do the job. Only light pressure is needed. Let the bristles cool before you unwrap the brush.

1075 When painting old woodwork, fill in the holes or cracks with a mixture of flour and some of the paint you are using. It hardens like cement and matches perfectly.

1076 When painting stairs, paint every other step first. When these are dry, paint the rest.

1077 To avoid cleaning paint brushes and rollers if you intend to use the same color later, or if you do not have time to clean immediately, place the brushes and rollers in a plastic bag, tie shut and place in the freezer. They will keep for several days without drying up.

1078 Protect hands from paint solvent by putting the brush and solvent into a strong plastic bag. With hands outside the bag, work the solvent into the brush through the plastic.

1079 After cleaning your paint brush, a few drops of oil worked into the bristles will leave the brush soft and ready to use.

1080 To clean paint rollers, fill an empty one-quart milk carton with solvent, put the roller inside and crimp the ends shut. Give the carton a few shakes, then let sit for a couple of hours.

1081 Simmer hardened paint brushes in full-strength vinegar. Remove the softened paint with a wire comb or brush.

1082 To remove oil or enamel paint from your hands, rub on paste floor wax and then wash with plenty of soap and warm water. There is no odor and it's easier on the skin than paint remover.

HANDY PERSON TIPS

HANDY PERSON TIPS

1083 In time, a partly used can of paint will develop a skin on top. To prevent this, cut waxpaper the size of the can and drop it in.

1084 To save partial cans of leftover paint, fill the airspace with a lightly inflated balloon before pressing on the lid.

1085 A coat of penetrating stain applied to a smooth wood surface may last only three or four years, but a second application after the wood has weathered will last as long as 10.

1086 To give bathroom fixtures a new look, paint with an epoxy paint, sold especially for that purpose.

1087 Never stir varnish. It has no color pigments which need blending and stirring will create air bubbles which can ruin a smooth finish.

1088 To frost a bathroom or garage window, make a solution of one cup of beer to four tbsp. Epsom salts and paint on the window. It washes off when you want a clear pane again.

1089 After wallpapering or painting, write the amount under a light-switch plate and you'll always know how much wallpaper or paint you need for that room.

1090 If you have a small hole in your wall (after moving pictures etc.) take a wax crayon as near the color of your wall as possible. Rub the hole with the crayon, polish with a dry cloth and the hole is invisible.

1091 Clean out old nail polish bottles and fill with 'touch-up' paint for scuffs and scratches that may occur on your walls.

1092 When hanging pictures on plaster walls, put a small piece of adhesive tape where the nail is to go in. Drive the nail through the tape. This helps prevent the plaster from cracking.

1093 To remove old wallpaper, first pull off as much as you can, then soak the remaining with Fleecy. It will peel off easily.

1094 Before wallpapering a wall, apply a coat of clear varnish to any grease spots. This will prevent the grease from soaking through the new paper.

1095 Instead of applying wallpaper with a sponge, dip a paint roller in the solution, squeeze slightly to prevent dripping and roll it over 20-30 sq. feet at a time.

1096 Buy stair carpeting a little longer than needed. When it shows signs of wear it can be shifted downward to delay replacement.

1097 To avoid wearing out spots on heavy traffic areas, use extra pieces of material cut out of the same material as the rug or linoleum.

1098 If your kitchen cupboards have worn out or if there are scuff marks around the handles, remove handles and glue on tiles to cover the scuffs. Replace handles over the tiles. This adds an interesting color accent and saves replacing or refinishing the doors.

1099 When a drain is clogged with grease, pour a cup of salt and a cup of baking soda into the drain, followed by a kettle of boiling water.

1100 If your water taps have a tendency to freeze during a cold spell, leave your taps on slightly. Running water will not freeze.

1101 Frozen water pipes can safely and easily be thawed out by using an ordinary hair dryer nozzle directed at the frozen pipe.

HANDY PERSON TIPS

HANDY PERSON TIPS

1102 To tighten cane-bottomed chairs, turn them upside down and liberally apply hot water to the underside. Dry the chairs in the sun.

1103 When sanding or refinishing, cover your hand with an old nylon stocking. Glide your hand over the surface to be re-done. Any rough areas will snag the stocking where more sanding needs to be done.

1104 To restore odor to an old cedar chest or closet, sandpaper lightly. This reopens pores in the wood to restore breathing.

1105 Spring-type clothespins are useful as clamps to hold light-weight glued materials together.

1106 To find a wall stud, hold a pocket compass level with the floor and at a right angle to the wall. Slowly move it along the surface of the wall. Movement of the compass will indicate the presence of nails and reveal stud location.

1107 You always have a measuring tape in your pocket—a U.S. dollar bill is 6 1/8 inches long and 2 5/8 inches wide.

1108 Stop drawers from sticking by running a candle along the tops.

1109 Use nonstick vegetable spray to lubricate squeaky hinges and sticky locks.

1110 Loosen rusted nuts or bolts with a few drops of ammonia or peroxide.

1111 To help remove stubborn nuts and bolts, pour on some cola soft drink.

1112 You can retrieve a broken key by putting some strong metal adhesive on the handle and holding it to the part stuck in the lock. Hold it there until the glue has set. When it holds, pull out the key. Don't use the key again.

1113 Four or five mothballs in your toolbox will keep the tools from rusting.

1114 A piece of chalk or charcoal in your toolbox will attract moisture and keep your tools from rusting.

1115 Save your old nuts, bolts and washers. They make excellent sinkers for your fishing line.

1116 Use discarded milk cartons, with the tops cut off, to store items in the workshop. Great for nails, screws etc.

1117 If one of your saucepan lids is missing a knob, put a screw through the hole with the point upwards and push a cork down onto it.

1118 To store a handsaw safely, cover the teeth with a split length of old garden hose.

1119 To sharpen scissors, fold a piece of aluminum foil three times, then cut through it several times with your scissors.

1120 Electrical cords from kitchen appliances are easy to find when stored in cardboard tubes from disposable towels. Color code the end of the tube if you have more than one in a drawer.

1121 Tuck electric appliance cords and extension cords into toilet tissue tubes, labelling each by length and by which cord fits which appliance.

1122 To keep cords of curling irons and blow dryers together in a drawer, use ponytail holders.

HANDY PERSON TIPS

HANDY PERSON TIPS

1123 To remove broken lightbulbs with ease, put switch into off position, then push a raw potato into the base and twist the broken bulb out.

1124 To get a broken lightbulb out of the socket, turn the switch off, then stick a soft bar of soap into the jagged edges of glass and use the soap as a handle to unscrew it easily and safely.

1125 If your flashlight batteries are getting weak while on a camping trip and you cannot replace them immediately, set them in the bright sunlight during the day and they will be temporarily rejuvenated.

1126 The charcoal in a rangehood filter can be recharged by placing it in a 450-degree oven for 30 minutes after cleaning the metal frame.

1127 When mailing fragile items, pack the excess space in the box with popped popcorn to insulate the package against damage/breakage.

1128 To allow sliding windows or drawers to move easier, use a bar of soap to grease tracks or runners.

1129 When a pin or needle won't penetrate an article, rub pin or needle in your hair and try again.

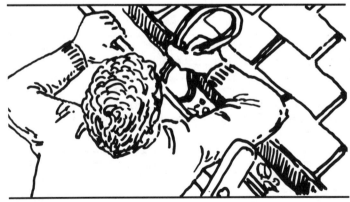

1130 A discarded fan belt from the car makes an ideal gutter-cleaning tool. Being flexible, yet firm, this belt is easily formed to shape the bottom of the gutter which enables muck and leaves to be scraped out without scratching the paint inside the gutter.

1131 Why climb a ladder? Use binoculars to get a closer look.

1132 Your ladder won't sink into soft earth if you place each leg into an empty coffee can or paint can.

1133 Use old or leftover linoleum to cover seats and tops of picnic tables.

1134 Small holes in window screens can be repaired by dabbing the hole with successive layers of clear nail polish.

1135 Put an extra house key in a water-tight container or plastic bag and store outside the house in the flower bed, under a rock etc. so you will never be locked out.

1136 Use extra-large plastic garbage bags as inexpensive protective covers for folding lawn furniture. This allows furniture to be stored outdoors without damage.

1137 Snow will slide off a shovel which has been sprayed with furniture polish or vegetable oil.

1138 Rub your snow shovel with parawax or candle wax before using. Even wet snow will slide off without buildup, keeping the shovel light and easy to manoeuvre.

1139 Use your fertilizer spreader to scatter sand on icy walkways.

1140 To remove dangerous ice off your steps, sprinkle with salt.

1141 Kitty litter can be used to de-ice your sidewalks and steps.

1142 Throw salt on fireplace logs once a month to prevent soot in the fireplace.

1143 To prevent your fireplace from smoking, raise the fire grate by placing bricks under the legs.

1144 Save your Nabob coffee bags to burn in the fireplace. Roll up tightly and then watch the varicolored flames when the bags are burned.

1145 To add a little color to your campfire, soak pinecones in a solution of ½ gallon water and ½ pound Borax. When dry, they burn a vivid green.

HANDY PERSON TIPS

HANDY PERSON TIPS

1146 To make your Christmas tree last longer, add sugar to the water.

1147 To preserve your Christmas tree longer, add Pinesol to the water.

1148 To fireproof the Christmas tree, mix eight oz. boracic acid in one gallon of water. Spray mixture over tree and let dry.

1149 To clean automobile chrome, rub with dampened aluminum foil.

1150 Add one cup of kerosene to the wash water when washing the car. Wipe well with a soft cloth — no rinsing is necessary. This will prevent rust and water will actually bead on the car during a rainfall.

1151 Wash your car with liquid dishwashing detergent. It won't scratch the surface.

1152 Windshield wipers smearing? Clean the windshield and wiper blade with rubbing alcohol.

1153 Make your own windshield washer fluid by combining one quart rubbing alcohol, one cup water and two Tblsp. liquid detergent.

1154 Use steel wool pads on your tire white side walls to keep them new looking.

1155 Keep open cans of motor oil clean by sealing them with the plastic lids from one-pound tins of coffee.

1156 A sheet of fabric softener under your car seat will keep the car smelling fresh.

1157 To clean corrosion from battery posts, make a paste of baking soda and water (paste should be thickness of cream). Brush on posts, leave for 10 minutes and brush off with water. Wipe dry with a rag. This leaves the posts and battery clean.

1158 Before leaving on holidays or a weekend trip in the summer, spray the front of your car with cooking oil (such as Pam). This will keep the bugs from sticking to the grill. Those that do will wash off with ease.

1159 Run your car air-conditioner five minutes weekly during the winter months to keep it in good condition.

1160 Prevent car doors from freezing by wiping the rubber gaskets with vegetable oil to seal out water.

1161 If your car door locks freeze, use your hairdryer to thaw them out.

1162 If door locks are frozen and a hairdryer is not available, heat the key with a lighter or match.

1163 To avoid having your car extension cord stolen, buy a somewhat longer cord, plug it in and, with the extra length, loop it and put it inside the door and close it. An alternative is to drive the front wheel over the cord.

1164 Your car block heater may be plugged in but the current may not be getting through. To make certain it is, wire in an inexpensive circuit test into the receptacle end of the heater cord. When you see the glow, you know the current is getting through.

1165 Be prepared for winter driving by purchasing a strip of expanded metal about eight inches wide and 24 inches long. (This is a diamond-patterned screen that can be purchased at most tin smith shops.) When placed under the wheels of your vehicle, it can get you out of most spots.

HANDY PERSON TIPS

HANDY PERSON TIPS

1166 If your car is stuck in snow, your floor mats or an old carpet, stored in the trunk, can be placed under the rear wheels for traction.

1167 Save old milk cartons and fill with sand to carry in your car in case you get stuck in the snow.

1168 Fill old milk cartons with old melted candles and/or parawax, insert a wick and keep in the trunk of your car in case of winter emergency.

1169 When travelling in the winter be prepared. Carry in your trunk a couple of plastic pails of dry sand, one small shovel, sleeping bags, a well-charged flashlight, outdoor extension cord and a couple of pairs of heavy wool socks (you can always use socks on your hands but it is difficult to put gloves on your feet). Always make certain that your gas tank is above the half-full mark.

1170 Preserve your garage floor, particularly in the winter, by placing carpet remnants on the area where the tires come in contact with the floor.

1171 To remove grease and oil stains from concrete, first scrape off as much of the stain as possible with a putty knife. Wet down the stains and sprinkle on TSP crystals (Trisodium Phosphate Crystals which can be purchased from most hardware stores). As the crystals dissolve, use a bristle brush and work on the stain for 15-20 minutes. Add a little more TSP and brush the spot vigorously. Mop up stain with clean water.

1172   Here are ways to remove oil stains on your driveway. For fresh stains, sprinkle kitty litter, grind in with your foot, let it absorb the oil, then sweep up. For older stains, use Spray N Wash, let stand approximately five minutes, then sprinkle on laundry detergent, scrub with stiff broom, then hose down. For really tough stains, use oven spray, let set and rinse with clear water.

HANDY PERSON TIPS

DONORS

Aldridge, Irene, Regina
Ames, Stewart, Yorkton
Anwender, Amelia, Regina
Avery, Donna, Oxbow
Baker, Denise, Raymore
Bakken, Beulah, Balgonie
Bakkel, Marg, Shaunavon
Baliko, Joan, Regina
Bandet, Roland, Regina
Barton, Darlene, Regina
Beattie, Joy, Swift Current
Bechdoldt, Lynne, Regina
Beckstead, Eleanor, Creelman
Becker, Mrs. O., Rocanville
Behr, R., Estevan
Beke, Della Rose, Regina
Belisle, Julie, Wauchope
Belbeck, Bernice, Rockglen
Bengert, Marla, Regina
Benz, Brian, Regina
Benz, Marilyn, Regina
Bencharski, Gwen, Elfros
Berkes, Winnifred, Whitewood
Berube, Sam, Regina
Berling, Doreen, Regina
Best, Mrs. B., Balgonie
Billingsley, Mrs. D., Regina
Billingsley, Jess, Regina
Bilan, Flo, Preeceville
Bilan, H., Preeceville
Bissett, Joan, Regina
Biyak, Kathy, Regina
Blackwood, Lillian, Regina
Blancher, Janet, Regina
Bleachley, Gordon, Pilot Butte
Bleackley, B., Swift Current
Blumhagen, Jean, Regina
Boa, Mae, Regina
Bodnarchuk, Mrs. Sonya, Canora
Boechler, Sandra, Regina
Bolton, Linda, Ceylon
Bonneau, Paul L., Gravelbourg
Boyd, Ruth, Regina
Bray, Teresa, McLean
Brewer, Tom, Regina
Bressler, Norma, Regina
Brentnell, E.R., Belle Plaine
Broad, Shirley, Melville
Bruener, Rudy, White City
Budd, Marrella, Regina
Bulych, Lydia, Ituna
Burr, Wendy, Weyburn
Burns, Sue, Regina
Campbell, Mrs. D.H., Pitt Meadows, B.C.
Campbell, Agnes, Regina
Carr, Kay, Shaunavon
Caswell, Helen, Moose Jaw
Cave, Mrs. W., Regina

Cave, Kathleen, Shaunavon
Celentano, Sandra, Regina
Chatterton, Robyn, Wolseley
Chase, Marilyn M.D., Moose Jaw
Chopty, Marlene, Preeceville
Christenson, Jean, Estevan
Clark, Ms. Rae, Maple Clark
Clairmont, L., Esterhazy
Clarke, Kathleen, Wolseley
Clarke, Mrs. A., Avonlea
Clarkson, Lois, Redvers
Colton, Lily E., Manor
Cole, Marg, Regina
Cooney, Mrs. Marg, Glen Ewen
Cook, Bryan, Esterhazy
Cooney, Marg, Glen Ewen
Costea, Patricia, Regina
Costron, Judy, Regina
Couprie, Rose, Regina
Crawford, L., Pilot Butte
Culbertson, P., Welwyn
Curtis, Suzanne, Wolseley
Dahl, Mrs. Muriel, Regina
Dartige, Diane, Whitewood
Deaust, Dianne, Regina
Deadlock, Anna, Estevan
Delsnider, Ken, Regina
Demchuk, Anne, Regina
Dereninsky, Elaine, Regina
Dereninsky, Allan, Saskatoon
Dereniwsky, Larry, Esterhazy
Dereniwsky, Kevin, Saskatoon
Derksen, Clara, Swift Current
Dewhurst, Laurie, Regina
Dewar, Trudy, Regina
Digney, Eva, Raymore
Dillistone, Gareth, Regina
Dillistone, Patricia, Regina
Dmyterko, Diane, Regina
Dorais, Marian, Regina
Doreau, Greg, Regina
Dukart, Mrs. Jean, Estevan
Dumonceaux, Harvey, Kipling
Dunn, Nancy, Moose Jaw
Dunn, Eve, Regina
Dunger, Leona, Regina
Dusterbeck, Jo, Regina
Dwyer, Leona, Regina
Eagles, Barbara A., Regina
Eaket, Agnes, Kenosee
Eberle, Marlene, Regina
Eberle, Mrs. E., Regina
Eddy, Kathleen, Foam Lake
Edwards, John, Regina
Elchuk, Darlene, Regina
Entner, Heather, Regina
Erfle, Anita, Regina
Erhardt, Lenore, Strasbourg

Erickson, Peggy, Strasburgh
Erickson, Judi, Radville
Evelt, Rosemarie, Regina
Fahlman, Peggy, Regina
Faller, Ruth, Southey
Farrell, Dianna, Regina
Fazakas, Lorrie, Cupar
Fee, D., Regina
Finch, Cora, Regina
Fisher, Helen, Moose Jaw
Fisher, Norma, Regina
Flaman, Ruby, Regina
Floen, Mrs. E., Oxbow
Fodey, Dolores, Regina
Foord, Janet, Macoun
Ford, Rose, Central Butte
Fraser, Barb, Regina
Fraser, David, Regina
Francis, Alma, Regina
Froehlich, Dora, Marquis
Froehlich, Lois, Regina
Froehlich, Bud, Marquis
Fulcher, Mrs. Orlean, Regina
Galbiati, Vicki, Regina
Ganje, Mrs. Bella, Estevan
Ganshorn, Barb, Regina
Garner, Gloria, Arcola
Gibson, Josephine, Regina
Gibson, Mrs. Lois, Regina
Gibbons, Donna, Weyburn
Ginter, Marion, Swift Current
Glaspey, Mrs. James, Oxbow
Goeres, Isabel, Weyburn
Gorniak, Ev, Regina
Gorrill, Mrs. Brenda, Regina
Gosselin, Marion, Regina
Gottselig, Marie, Balgonie
Grant, Mrs. Barbara, Estevan
Grady, Barbara, Estevan
Gress, Joan, Regina
Gress, Matt, Regina
Greggain, Lorna, Regina
Green, Christine, Craven
Groff, Glenn, Regina
Hack, Mrs. G., Regina
Hack, H., Regina
Hackewich, Mary, Regina
Hala, Gertrude, Regina
Hammett, Cheryl, Regina
Handy, Mrs. Sharon, Calgary, Alta.
Harker, Kay, Regina
Harty, Brenda, Regina
Harper, Irene, Redvers
Hastings, Edith A., Regina Beach
Hawryluk, Barbara, Kamsack
Haywood, Bernie, Regina
Heath, Heather, Regina
Hehn, Mrs. Alice, Regina

Heidinger, Helen, Arcola
Heilman, Jane, Moose Jaw
Heibein, Eileen, Zehner
Heisler, Helen, Regina
Henderson, Teresa, Gainsborough
Herperger, Cheryl, Regina
Hilt, Merelyn, Regina
Hill, Scott, Pangman
Himmelspeck, Neil, Regina
Hodgson, Lill, Regina
Hotcher, Irene, Regina
Huber, Eunice, Lipton
Huber, Eunice, Lipton
Hugel, Caroline, Regina
Hutchen, Irene, Regina
Irwin, Mary, Estevan
James, Beverly, Swift Current
Janowski, Jean, Weyburn
Jawoski, Jean, Regina
Johnson, A.D., Regina
Johnson, Mrs. E. M., Regina
Johnson, Sheila, Gainsborough
Jolly, Mrs. Lois, Regina
Jones, Irene M., Edgeley
Jones, Patricia, Weyburn
Jones, Sharon, Weyburn
Josin, Mrs. Freda, Regina
Kahon, Shirley, Regina
Kalynuk, Mrs. G., Canora
Kambeitz, Gailene, Regina
Kaytor, Joan, Regina
Keene, Mrs. Agnes, Regina
Kegel, Georgina, Pilot Butte
Kelln, Emma, Semans
Kemery, Noreen, Kipling
Kennedy, Ann, Newport
Kennedy, Ann Marie, Regina
Kennedy, Freda, McLean
Kines, Helena, Roblin, Man.
Kippan, Anna, Regina
Klemp, Edith, Pense
Kness, Kathy, Regina
Knibbs, Mrs. Susan, Carnduff
Knoblauch, Vi, Griffin
Konoff, Mrs. Mariann, Regina
Konoff, Mrs. Bunny, Regina
Krause, Mrs. J., Regina
Krentz, Caroline D., Regina
Krushkowski, Anne, Kamsack
Krueger, Glenn, Shaunavon
Kunz, Betty, Regina
Kuyek, Dale, Regina
Laing, George, Swift Current
Laing, Alma, Swift Current
Lambord, Marie, Estevan
Langenegger, Pat, McLean
Langenegger, Steve, McLean
Lang, Dorothy, Chamberlain

Langelotz, Sighilde, Regina
Lapiere, Donna, Regina
Lareau, Lill, Regina
Laurans, Irene, Regina
Lawrence, Mrs. Lily, Regina
Leggett, Mrs. R.I., Kipling
Lehmann, Katherine, Regina
Lepoudre, Faith, Balgonie
Levenick, Elsie, Regina
Lewko, Kathy, Regina
Linnell, Jean, Summerberry
Linnell, Joe, Summerberry
Liski, G., Regina
Longworth, Darlene, Regina
Loos, Ron, Yellow Grass
Lott, Shirley, Regina
Love, Mrs. Jean, Moose Jaw
Lussier, Margaret, Regina
Macri, Mrs. Frank, Regina
Macknak, Georgina, Regina
MacLean, Marion, Melville
Mann, Eleanor, Grenfell
Mang, Mrs. Joyce, Pense
Marion, Merle, Davidson
Marshall, Gertrude, Melville
Mayes, Eleanor, Regina
McAllister, Diane, Maple Creek
McClelland, Elsie, Regina
McGrath, Delia, Regina
McGregor, Mrs. Nell, Central Butte
McGillicky, Julie Ann, Coronach
McLashen, Helen, Yorkton
McLafferty, Norma, Moose Jaw
Melle, Deb, Minton
Merriman, Doris, Regina
Metereo, Mrs. Jeannie, Regina
Miller, J., Estevan
Miller, Rose, Estevan
Miller, Robert, Regina
Mildenberger, Les, Sedley
Mildenberger, Mrs. Sally, Sedley
Minto, Sharlene, Regina
Minto, Garth, Regina
Mitchell, Douglas, Kamsack
Monteyne, Darlene, Estevan
Monroe, Beverly, Regina
Morris, Eileen, Gravelbourg
Morton, Laura, Kisbey
Mozylisky, Tony, Regina
Munro, Joyce, Swift Current
Murray, M., Regina
Murdoch, Mrs. Joyce, Shaunavon
Nehn, Mrs. Alice, Regina
Nelson, Mrs. Rose, Stockholm
Nelson, Nancy, Regina
Nelson, Mrs. Arlene, Wilcox
Nerby, Helen E., Indian Head
Nichol, Elizabeth, Swift Current

Noess, Edith, Assiniboia
Norman, B., Regina
Nording, Mrs. Carolyn, Regina
Ohashi, Mrs. A., Regina
Oleksinski, Mrs. E., Regina
Olson, Mrs. P., Sturgis
Orban, Luana, Regina
Orser, Christina, Regina
Orthner, Viola, Regina
Osolinski, Stan, Yorkton
Parker, Robert, Regina
Parker, Vic, Regina
Pask, Jean, Esterhazy
Pattison, Bonnie, Regina
Paterson, Donna, Edenwold
Peart, Christine, Regina
Peart, Betty Ann, Regina
Peel, Betty Ann, Regina
Pepin, Sharon, Regina
Perepiolkin, Fred, Swift Current
Perepiolkin, Susan, Swift Current
Perepiolkin, Winnie S., Swift Current
Peterson, Kathy, Regina
Peterson, Patti, Regina
Pickering, Shirley, Weyburn
Piluk, Miss Mary Jane, Estevan
Pinkering, P., Earl Grey
Popowich, Mary, Wynyard
Powley, Mrs. L., Regina
Powley, J.C., Regina
Powell, Bernice D., Yorkton
Powchuck, Mrs. Peter, Grenfell
Powchuck, Peter, Grenfell
Preikchat, Rose, White City
Predy, Ruth, Canora
Pritchard, D., Regina
Priddell, Shirley, Qu'Appelle
Procyk, Wanda, Montmartre
Procyk, Steven, Montmartre
Prosofsky, Tracey, Regina
Purvis, Donna, Carlyle
Purdy, Elaine, Tantallon
Rathgeber, Marie, Melville
Reed, Richard, Craven
Reget, Georgina, Pilot Butte
Reiss, Mrs. Atholine, Indian Head
Relke, Jane, Regina
Relkey, Pauline, Regina
Rempel, Janis, Regina
Reynard, Terry, Regina
Reynard, Edna, Regina
Rezansoff, Penny, Kamsack
Riddell, Mrs. E., Regina
Robin, C., Regina
Robb, Norma Jean, Fort Qu'Appelle
Robillard, Della, Fort Qu'Appelle
Rodine, Harold, Weyburn
Rollins, Tim, Regina

DONORS

Rollins, Leslie, Regina
Ross, Louise, Regina
Ross, Louise, Cymric
Russel, M. June, Craven
Ryan, Janet, Tantallon
Sali, Claudia, Regina
Sapara, Mrs. Donald, Esterhazy
Sawchyn, Jean, Melville
Sayer, Pat, Regina
Sayer, Pat, Regina
Schneider, Tilly, Regina
Schuck, Marilyn, Weyburn
Schmidt, E.J., Regina
Schmidt, Diane, Regina
Schinbein, Beryl, Cabri
Schroeder, Mrs. Beulah, Chamberlain
Schuck, Mrs. L. Pearl, Regina
Schick, Palma, Regina
Schick, Norm, Regina
Schatz, E., Regina
Schomburg, Mrs. F., Montmartre
Scott, Dorothy, Fillmore
Scott, Lorraine, Regina
Segal, B., Fort Qu'Appelle
Serfling, Donna, Regina
Shea, Barb, Regina
Shul, Wendy, Regina
Simmons, J., Regina
Smyth, Pat, Regina
Snell, Muriel, Regina
Sokulski, Don, Regina
Solomon, Mary, Regina
Souillet, Jeannine, Fort Qu'Appelle

Spence, Frances, Indian Head
Spence, Duncan, Indian Head
Springett, Margaret, Moose Jaw
Stakiw, Gail, Regina
Staite, John A., Regina
Stewart, Olive, Fort Qu'Appelle
Stillwell, Joyce, Regina
Stockton, Marie, Regina
Strandlund, Martha, Broadview
Swanson, C., Regina
Szabo, Mrs. Marge, Regina
Tarr, Maria, Wolseley
Tetlow, Celine, Regina
Thomas, Vi, Weyburn
Thomson, Mrs. M., Regina
Thoreson, E., Moose Jaw
Thurmeier, Mrs. B., Regina
Tokevich, Mrs. I., Regina
Tokevich, Mrs. S., Regina
Trafananko, Mrs. Helen, Regina
Trafananko, R.J., Regina
Turcotte, Lynne, Regina
Turner, M., Regina
Urbanoski, Joyce, Yorkton
Van de Wyer, Doreen, Halbrite
Van Dresar, Leila E., Regina
Vincze, Maryann, Kipling
Waldbauer, Bob, Regina
Wasylyshen, Mrs. Carol, Yorkton
Watkins, Ron, Fort Qu'Appelle
Webb, Mrs. M., Regina
Weimer, Shirley, Kendal
Weir, Hazel, Regina

Weir, Mrs. Willian, Arcola
Weisberger, Joann, Estevan
Whitney, Gayle, Regina
Wiebe, L., Regina
Wielyoz, Bernice, Moosomin
Wild, Juanita, Regina
Williams, Shirley, Regina
Wild, Isobelle, Regina
Wilson, Mrs. Doreen, Lang
Winsor, Carol, Regina
Woods, Adeline, Swift Current
Woroniak, Lorraine, Wawota
Yaholnitsky, T.P., Regina
Yemen, Dorothy, Regina
Young, Mrs. Iris, Regina
Young, Arrol, Arcola
Yurkowski, Melinda, Regina
Zacharri, Sylvia, Prince Albert
Zacharri, William, Prince Albert
Zacharki, Mrs. Sylvia, Prince Albert
Zak, Annette, Fir Mountain
Zander, Dennis, Wauchope
Zatylny, Vera, Dysart
Zazada, Jo, Regina
Zimmer, Sharon, Regina
Zimmerman, Kathy, Regina
Zimmerman, Elsie, Regina
Zimmerman, Jeanne, Regina
Zora, E.E., L'Arche
Zrymiak, Gail, Ituna
Zurburg, Sandra, Esterhazy
Zyla, Rosella, Fillmore

In the long process of sorting and editing hundreds of readers' tips, some names and tips were inadvertently separated from each other and it became impossible to match them up.

Thus there may be a few names missing from the list of donors, and The Leader-Post Carrier Foundation would like to apologize for anyone missed, and to thank all who submitted tips to The Leader-Post and thus to this publication.

INDEX

INDEX

INDEX

Publications from Blue Sky Marketing, Inc.

The Family Memory Book: Highlights of Our Times Together, by Judy Lawrence. This beautiful, fill-in-the-blank book captures and preserves, for lifelong enjoyment, five full years of keepsake personal memories by helping you to effortlessly record the highlights of holidays, special events and other occasions. The simple, step-by-step process motivates even readers who have long wanted to record these special events, but haven't known how or where to start. Hardcover, $14.95*, 7x10, 96 pages.

The Home Owner's Journal: What I Did & Where I Did It, by Colleen Jenkins. Stop playing Hide and Seek with your home decorating and repair records. This journal lets you keep all your important home details at your fingertips! You'll know how much paint it took to do the kitchen the last time and when something was last cleaned, serviced, or repaired. Simply fill in the blanks as it guides you step by step. Save yourself money, time, and frustration by recording everything in ONE place. Delightfully illustrated, fill-in-the-blank book. Spiral binding, $9.95*, 136 pages, 6x9

Vacation Getaway—A Journal For Your Travel Memories, by Bruce Moulton. This unique journal makes it easy for travelers to record the daily highlights and expenses of their trips. It features 14 top-opening pocket pages for storing receipts, postcards, photographs, and other mementos for each day—all in a remarkably compact and easy-to-carry size. Plus, the spiral binding allows it to lie flat for easy writing. Also included are practical travel tips. Softcover, $6.95*, 5x9, 36 pages.

The Weekly Menu Planner & Shopping List. In one easy step, busy cooks can plan a week's worth of meals and have an organized shopping list ready for a *fast* trip to the market—all on one sheet. The top "Menu" portion is in calendar format and shows your family "what's cooking" that week; the bottom "Shopping List" portion helps you prepare your list for those meals quickly! Includes a year's supply of 52 sheets. It helps you get organized, shop faster, save money, and eat healthier. Charming country design. $6.95*, 8 1/2x11

Money and Time Saving Household Hints, by The Leader-Post Carrier Foundation Inc. Packed with over 1,000 clever, useful and sometimes startling solutions to everyday problems, this national best seller in Canada is now available in the USA for the first time! *Money & Time-Saving Household Hints* provides new solutions to everything from how to put the "bounce" back into old tennis balls to an astonishing way to make ferns grow faster! There's even an *entire chapter* devoted to "pantihose!" Softcover, $6.95*, 6x9, 128 pages.

*Prices effective 10/92 and are subject to change.

Blue Sky Marketing, Inc. P.O. Box 21583-S,
St. Paul, MN, 55121-1583, USA (612) 456-5602.

Turn Page For Order Form

ORDER FORM

**U.S. currency please, if ordering from outside the United States.
Check or credit card only. Please Print!**

__ Check enclosed. Charge my: __ Visa __ Mastercard __ Discover

Card # _____ Exp. Date _____

Signature _____

Name _____

Company (if applicable) _____

Street Address _____

      Reminder: To ship UPS we <u>must</u> have your <u>street</u> address.

City/State/ZIP _____

Special Shipping Instructions _____

Daytime Phone (for questions about your order) _____

Qty.	Title/Description	Price Per Item*	Total

Mail to: Merchandise Total _____

Blue Sky Marketing, Inc.   6.5% Tax (MN addresses only) _____

P.O. Box 21583-S   Shipping (see below) _____

St. Paul, MN 55121-1583   TOTAL _____

USA

To order by phone, call toll-free 1-800-444-5450

Shipping to U.S.A. Addresses

<u>If ordering</u>:
* 1 book, add $2.50 for U.S. Mail "book rate" (may take 4 weeks) or
    $3.50 for UPS.
* 2-4 books, UPS (or 1st Class Mail) for **only** $3.50!
* 5+ books, **FREE** shipping!!!
* Call or write for shipping charges to addresses outside the U.S.A.

*Prices effective 10/92 and are subject to change.